Why Our Churches Do Not Win Souls

By
Dr. John R. Rice, D.D., Litt.D.

Sword of the Lord Publishers
Murfreesboro, Tennessee

Printed and bound in U.S.A.

INTRODUCTION

Christian churches, local congregations of born-again believers, ought to win many souls. They ought to multiply themselves and grow rapidly, getting lost sinners to repent and trust Christ for salvation and, being born again, set out to live the Christian life. Sadly, I say that most of our churches win few souls, and many, many thousands win none at all! Let us face that sad condition honestly and acknowledge it, compare it with the New Testament standard for churches, then intelligently set out to find the basic failures which prevent soul winning and make our churches relatively fruitless and powerless to propagate Christianity and get people saved.

1. Let us define our terms. By <u>churches</u> we mean local congregations of Christians, as the term is usually used in the New Testament. Local congregations are the units through which Christian people have worked to win souls, usually. I speak not here of denominations. <u>Church</u> in the Bible never refers to a denomination, and no denominational organizations are pictured in the New Testament. At any rate, soul winning must be done on the ground level, as far as organized Christianity is concerned, souls are won by members of local churches and make their profession of faith and enlist to serve God, usually, in local congregations.

When we speak of winning souls, we mean bringing the Gospel to people who come to see themselves lost sinners, who trust Christ for salvation and thus are regenerated, born again, and become children of God. We speak now not of enlisting people for church membership, though we believe that after people are saved they should unite with local groups, be baptized, and work with other Christians to win souls and help one another. We mean what Paul the apostle meant in I Corinthians 9:22, "I am made all things to all men, that I might by all means save some." We mean what he meant in Romans 10:1-3: "Brethren, my heart's desire and prayer to God for Israel is, that they might be saved. For I bear them record that they have a zeal of God, but not according to knowledge. For they being ignorant of God's righteousness, and going about to establish their own righteousness, have not submitted themselves unto the righteousness of God." We believe that the Gospel that Christ died for our sins and rose again the third day according to the Scriptures, may be preached and witnessed to poor, unregenerate men. They may be taught to trust in Christ and so be instantly made children of God. We believe in Christian growth, but a baby must be born before it grows, and one must be made a child of God by regeneration before he grows in Christian grace. So our churches and our preachers and Christian people in the churches ought to win souls to Christ and have men born again, saved.

We need not emphasize that this is the historic Christian position, the obvious position of the New Testament. By winning souls we do not mean winning people to social causes. We do not mean changing society in general. Nor do we mean simply moral reform, though all these good ends come when men are changed in heart and made into children of God.

2. We should say plainly that soul winning is the business of every Christian and that souls are won by individuals, not by the church as a corporate body. The preacher from the pulpit may preach the Gospel with power and be used of God to save souls, but he is an individual. Both pastor and all other Christians should witness individually. The Sunday school teacher should win pupils in her class, but usually she will win them in personal conversation and witnessing and entreaty. The mother may win her child; the man may

win his neighbor. Andrew won his brother, Simon Peter, in John 1:41 and 42. Jesus won Nicodemus, we believe, in John 3. He won the woman at the well of Sychar in Samaria in John, chapter 4. Individuals are won by individuals.

3. But it is only fair to say that the climate and the occasion and the instruction and the preaching and teaching and training and the program that leads individual Christians to win souls are in some sense a united work. Some churches develop many, many soul winners, and all together win many souls. Some other churches, local congregations, have no soul winners, so the church as a whole does not see souls saved.

Thus, while we know the individual must be won by individual efforts, and often by more than one person, yet the standards, the climate and the program that make Christians into soul winners and make it possible for them to win souls, or at least make it easier, must grow in the churches. Churches can be made into soul-winning churches, or whole congregations can fail.

We seek in this book to find the basic causes of failure in soul winning in the churches.

John R. Rice

TABLE OF CONTENTS

These Pastors Concur

Drs. Lee Roberson, Jack Hyles, Tom Malone, Harold Sightler and Robert Gray, Who Pastor Great Soul-Winning Churches, Concur in This Book and Add Their Testimonies

On the Board of Directors and on the Co-operating Board of the Sword of the Lord Foundation are pastors of some of the greatest soul-winning churches in the world. I have asked some of these men to read the manuscript of this book, write their comments and suggestions, their approval or disapproval, and to give a word of testimony about the blessing of God on their own ministries. Since God has so graciously helped them to lead and build churches that win thousands of souls, their counsel is most valuable and we are glad to have them concur in the sentiments of this book.

Major, area-wide conferences on revival and soul winning are sponsored by the Sword of the Lord, where thousands of preachers and tens of thousands of people learn how to win souls, how to build an evangelistic church, how to have prayers answered, how to be filled with the Spirit for soul-winning power, how to put on a soul-winning visitation program. In such conferences these good men and others help us stir revival fires and teach how to bring back New Testament power and joy and results in Christian work.

I am deeply grateful for their co-operation and I am glad to give here their testimonies. The reader will do well to hear these notably used and Spirit-empowered men of God on the matter of building and leading soul-winning churches.

Dr. Lee Roberson is pastor of Highland Park Baptist Church, Chattanooga, Tennessee, with many thousands of members and forty-two chapels besides the main church and congregation; is president of Tennessee Temple Schools, director of Camp Joy and has an active and strong missionary program.

Dr. Jack Hyles is pastor of the First Baptist Church of Hammond, Indiana, with some six thousand members; is vice-president of the Sword of the Lord Foundation and Sword conference director.

Dr. Tom Malone is pastor of the Emmanuel Baptist Church, Pontiac, Michigan; president of Midwestern Seminary and Emmanuel Bible College.

Dr. Harold Sightler is pastor of the Tabernacle Baptist Church, Greenville, South Carolina; director of the Bright Spot radio chain broadcast; head of a Christian grammar school and a children's home.

Dr. Robert Gray, Jr., is pastor of the Trinity Baptist Church, Jacksonville, Florida.

Now hear their testimonies.

A Definite Aim

By Dr. Lee Roberson, Pastor
Highland Park Baptist Church
Chattanooga, Tennessee

Why do churches fail? Why do they fail in soul winning, in attendance, in missionary endeavors?

Answer: They lack a definite goal.

The business of the local church is soul winning. The business of the pastor, the song leader, the choir, the Sunday school, the youth organizations, is soul winning.

Twenty-three years in my ministry at Highland Park in Chattanooga we have had one single aim: To win men to Christ. This has been the purpose of the main church, the forty-two chapels, the Union Gospel Mission, Camp Joy, the radio ministry, the foreign mission program. Yes, and this is the purpose of Tennessee Temple Schools.

Every service of the church has an evangelistic emphasis. The sermon may be directed to Christians, but the conclusion will be to the unsaved. In every service of our church there is a response. We pray, we work, we witness, we expect God to move upon the hearts of men.

First, we emphasize a plan to reach people--visitation. Each week scores of our people visit throughout the city. The Thursday night visitation program is conducted in every season of the year.

Secondly, every service of the church is planned to present a plea for souls. When lost people are brought to church, we want them to hear the Gospel and to know that somebody cares.

Thirdly, an invitation is given at every hour--Sunday morning, Sunday evening, and Wednesday night. No service is wasted. All services are used to press the matter of salvation.

For more than fifteen years, over a thousand people per year have been baptized at the Highland Park Baptist Church. This year the number will go beyond the 1,500 mark. (Later we find Dr. Roberson baptized 1,734 converts this church year. J.R.R.) We have had many others saved, even hundreds, who have united with other churches. As I dictate this brief article, I am conscious of the precious hours on yesterday. Some sixty-two people in all walked the aisles. Most of them came by profession of faith. Some were people visiting in our church from out of the city. One fine young man from New York City came forward and accepted

Christ. A young lady from Norfolk, Virginia, came for salvation. She testified that she had been in Chattanooga only two hours at the time that she was saved.

Most of the people who respond to the public invitations have been won to Christ by our members previous to the service.

What is the definite aim of all of our work? To bring people to Christ! It was written of Andrew, "And he brought him [Simon Peter] to Jesus" (John 1:42). Soul winning is every Christian's business. We are to be in the "bringing" business.

The High Hour

By Dr. Jack Hyles, Pastor
First Baptist Church
Hammond, Indiana

I have read with interest this tremendous manuscript by Dr. Rice, Why Our Churches Do Not Win Souls. There is no doubt in my mind that this book will be the source of more Satanic opposition than any other book written by the Twentieth Century's Mightiest Pen. The fact that Satan will oppose it will be proof of its spiritual value. I am sure that it is one of the greatest works of Dr. Rice. I advise every pastor to read it carefully and open-mindedly, evaluating his ministry as he reads.

There are two observations that come to me as I think of this work. The first is, I doubt if any preacher will realize his evangelistic potential until he realizes the importance of evangelism in public worship. Second, no church can reach its soul-winning potential until it is organized for soul winning and stripped of the needless organization we find in our churches today.

The "high hour" of the First Baptist Church of Hammond, Indiana, is at 10:50 on Sunday morning. This is our evangelistic service for the week. Many years ago when America's population was largely rural, the Sunday evening service was better attended than the Sunday morning service. Because of this, the evening service was the evangelistic hour.

The trend in our generation has been toward larger Sunday morning crowds. Because of this, it is our feeling that Sunday morning is the best time to have the evangelistic service. To be sure, there are more prospects there and a greater need for the preaching of the Gospel.

All we do in our church points toward this hour. The Sunday School, the Training Union, the W.M.S., the Visitation Program, the Youth Program, the Music Program, and all of our activities are pointed toward a great harvest of souls during the invitation following the Sunday morning message.

We operate twenty bus routes, bringing from 450 to 850 people a Sunday to Sunday school and preaching. Every Sunday people are saved from these bus routes. We have many other visitation programs (our ladies' visitation program, our youth visitation program, our regular visitation teams, etc.) which all point toward the Sunday morning invitation. Every Sunday people come forward who are won to Christ on the visitation programs. We operate a rescue mission. Every Sunday people come forward from this phase of our ministry. We employ a full-time worker with the deaf and handicapped. Nearly every Sunday we reap from this phase of our church program.

Each week our teachers and officers give a report of their visitation and soul winning for the past week. It is a very, very rare Sunday when several teachers and officers do not bring someone to the Lord Jesus Christ during the invitation. Our church staff of full-time workers turns in a weekly report concerning its soul-winning activities. Last year an average of ten people a Sunday came forward during the invitation who had been won to Christ by members of the staff.

When a person in our area passes away, his family receives a gospel witness from the First Baptist Church. When a couple gets married, they receive a note of congratulation, along with a gospel witness, from the First Baptist Church. This is also true in the case of every family who has a baby and every person who has a wreck, has a fire, receives an honor, etc. Many of these people come forward during the public services on Sunday morning.

The activities listed above are only a few of the many activities that point toward the "high hour" on Sunday morning.

This program has resulted in tremendous blessings from God. Every Sunday many people come to the Lord Jesus Christ and trust Him as Saviour. During the past twelve months over 1,700 people have walked the aisles of our church in response to the public invitation at the close of each sermon, receiving Christ or transferring their membership. We have baptized converts every Sunday morning and every Sunday evening for many months.

Now of course there are other benefits from such a program. This has enabled our Sunday school to increase from 700 a Sunday to over 2,000 a Sunday in the past four years. It has made it possible for our financial receipts to triple in the last five years. We believe that many of the things that churches spend most of their time on would be even more successful as a by-product in a church that makes its big job the winning of souls to Jesus Christ.

Someone said while visiting our church recently that if a church had a program set up like ours, anybody could pastor a church like that. I told him, "You are exactly right." The greatness of our church is not because of the greatness of the preacher or the greatness of the sermons, but be-

cause of the greatness of the people who are scattered a-
broad everywhere preaching the Gospel and who are daily
in the temple and in every house ceasing not to teach and
preach Jesus Christ.

There is no worship so sweet both to God and to the spiritual Christian as the worship we enjoy as we reap on Sunday morning what we have sown during the week. This worship makes the Sunday morning service truly the "high
hour."

"The Basic Fundamentals of New Testament Christianity"

By Dr. Tom Malone, Pastor
Emmanuel Baptist Church
Pontiac, Michigan

I have enjoyed reading the manuscript for the book, Why Our Churches
Do Not Win Souls. It is a much-need-
ed book because it points out the condition of fundamental churches today
which do not win souls. It gets down
to the basic fundamentals of New Testament Christianity, which must be
emphasized and practiced if souls are
to be saved daily and consistently in
our churches. I endorse and thank God
for this book with all my heart. Every preacher in America must read it!

Our church, Emmanuel Baptist, averages over 1,500 in
Sunday school in the main church alone. Seven other churches in the Pontiac area alone have been founded, fostered and

supported during the past twelve years. In these churches there is an average of 1,700 in Sunday school each Sunday. A periodical report of these churches and Emmanuel Baptist Church shows more than fifty conversions per week and twenty-five baptisms per week.

Emmanuel Baptist Church has an average of twelve candidates for baptism per week and over 600 additions to the church per year for the past six years.

In June and July of 1965 in the Emmanuel Baptist Church, there have been 165 professions of faith in the Lord Jesus Christ.

"Completely and Scripturally"

By Dr. Harold B. Sightler, Pastor
Tabernacle Baptist Church
Greenville, South Carolina

I have carefully read this manuscript. It is great. I cannot remember having ever seen anything in print on this needy subject and theme. You have covered the subject completely and scripturally.

The chapter on formalism as a hindering factor is great. I feel this has proven the ruin of many Southern Baptist churches and many independents.

The chapter on church music is verified by the church I am now in as I write this letter--The Gospel Light Baptist Church, Walkertown, North Carolina, Rev. Bobby Roberson, pastor. This church baptized 146 converts last year to lead the state of North Carolina. Their music is informal.

I personally appreciate the chapter on Sunday school, too. As a pastor, I have found this door most effective in reaching the lost. At Tabernacle, we do our visitation through the Sunday school. Our four buses have been used these fourteen years to bring in many of those who had no other way to come. Many of these have been saved.

This new book will be greatly used of God.

"Diagnosis Accurate, Fair, a Classic"

By Dr. Bob Gray, Pastor
Trinity Baptist Church
Jacksonville, Florida

After reading carefully the manuscript of <u>Why Our Churches Do Not Win Souls</u>, I was profoundly impressed by two observations that came immediately to mind.

First, the tremendous analysis that Dr. Rice has made as to why our churches are not winning souls is a classic! After preaching for years in revival meetings and Bible conferences across the country, I have learned firsthand that his diagnosis is accurate and fair. Secondly, the very determined adherence of the author to scriptural principle and practice for soul winning made me feel as if I had been using this new and recently written volume as a handbook for years! And how I thank God for many new and fresh insights that I gleaned from reading this very practical manual. If only preachers and soul-conscious laymen will read and prayerfully study this book, what a tremendous revival could sweep over the evangelical churches of our land.

Perhaps the simple testimony of Trinity Baptist Church in Jacksonville, Florida, will serve to confirm the conclusions of this book and challenge the heart of some pastor, evangelist, or Sunday school worker. It was through the contact that God afforded me years ago in the first Sword of the Lord Bible Conference at Toccoa, Georgia, that I learned of the availability and necessity of Holy Spirit power in which to serve the Lord and win souls for Him. Forsaking all desire and ambitions for denominational recognition, I determined that I wanted the breath of God, the fullness of Holy Spirit power upon my life and ministry regardless of the cost! By the time I was called as pastor to the Trinity Baptist Church, I knew that the Bible pattern for soul winning and a spiritual ministry was the only route to great blessings from the Lord.

Eleven years ago our church was a typical Southern Baptist church, with a very strong emphasis on the denominational program and no soul-winning ministry beyond the preaching ministry of the pastor. Sunday school attendance was around 250, and less than 100 came out for Training Union. During the year previous to our coming, less than twenty-five baptisms had been recorded. The services were formal, even for a small church, and many holding office in the church were worldly and unspiritual. Incorporating the very methods and New Testament philosophy that Dr. Rice has espoused in this book, I set out, under God, to build a Bible-preaching, Scripture-practicing, New Testament church at Trinity. I shall never cease to be grateful to God for the faithful and precious people who have stood with me through the years to accomplish this goal in our city.

To the glory of God, our church has led the local Jacksonville Baptist Association for the last ten consecutive years in baptisms and has also led the Florida Baptist Convention for five of those years in the number of people saved and baptized! Our Sunday school attendance is now averaging over 1,100 and Training Union attendance over 700, and we usually average over 600 in the Wednesday evening prayer meeting service. The dear Lord was gracious to us this past year by permitting us to baptize 351 converts...just fourteen short of our yearly goal. It seems to me that we ought to strive for New Testament results, "adding unto the church daily," since we are using New Testament methods.

In order to reach as many people as possible with the Gospel, my faithful people at Trinity have joined with me to sponsor a daily 30-minute radio broadcast, a downtown rescue mission, a monthly gospel paper, a full-time deaf ministry, seven Sunday school buses, our own summer youth camp facility, Sunday afternoon services for the city jail and local convalescent homes, eight missionaries who receive partial support from the church and eight who receive full-time support. Plans are now in the making for the establishment of a Christian bookstore and a Christian day-school program. Frankly, in view of the very poor and inadequate buildings of our present situation, nothing less than the Holy Spirit could have been responsible for the souls that have been saved and the growth that God has given in every phase of our ministry.

In a city of 500,000 and almost 200 Baptist churches, we believe that our spiritual future for Christ and soul winning is as bright as the promises of God!

1. The New Testament Pattern for Soul-Winning Churches

We will not be impressed with the tragic failure of our churches until we see them compared with the standards set in New Testament churches. A man who is a good citizen of respectable morals, who obeys the laws and supports his family, may appear to be a very fine man compared with a criminal or a bum. But put up beside the white righteousness of Jesus Christ and a new heart washed in the blood of Jesus, which God requires, he may find himself a depraved and doomed sinner. Compared with his neighbor, a man may be good, but compared with the Bible standard, he is shown to be a poor sinner who needs to be born again.

Just so a church with its lovely building, Gothic arches, stained glass windows, robed choirs, pipe organ music, and respectable members, with money given to the poor, and the preacher with his social righteousness, may be a fine church compared with another church in the same block. But compared to the churches in the New Testament, as revealed in the book of Acts, churches in which multiplied thousands were won to Christ in short years, the average church will find itself woefully inadequate, failing God and failing its community, and responsible for the blood of thousands of lost souls who ought to have been won!

I. The Standard Jesus Set: Try to Win "Every Creature"

What is the standard which the Lord Jesus set for us in this matter of winning souls? He said, "Go ye into all the world, and preach the gospel to every creature. He that believeth and is baptized shall be saved; but he that believeth not shall be damned" (Mark 16:15, 16). So the members of a local congregation should take the Gospel to every individual in their community and within reach. That is, the Lord Jesus commanded a saturation effort in soul winning.

Nearly everybody will agree that the Great Commission plan by the Saviour demands that soul winning have priority, that soul winning be the main business of Christians, pastors and churches. This is the "Great Commission." This sets out the principal plan the Lord Jesus had for His disciples after He went away. Then surely soul winning, in an effort to reach "every creature" with the saving Gospel, is the main business of Christians and churches.

Similarly, it is given in Matthew 28:19, 20: "Go ye therefore, and teach all nations, baptizing them in the name of the Father, and of the Son, and of the Holy Ghost: Teaching them to observe all things whatsoever I have commanded you: and, lo, I am with you alway, even unto the end of the world." Notice that teach here does not mean expounding the Scriptures to Christians. It means to make disciples. The Greek word is matheteuo, meaning to make a disciple. It is the word used for disciple in Matthew 27:57 about Joseph of Arimathaea. The feminine form is used for disciple for: "a certain disciple named Tabitha" in Acts 9:36. So, the first teaching commanded in the Great Commission is to make disciples, the teaching that leads them to be baptized.

Then after they are baptized we are commanded, "Teaching them to observe all things whatsoever I have commanded you." That is, the new converts now committed and baptized are taught to do the same things that we have all been commanded to do--to make disciples. Evidently, then, all New Testament Christians have the same command the apostles had. When Peter got somebody saved, he should urge him to be baptized. Then when a new convert is baptized, he should be taught to do exactly what Jesus told Peter to do. Surely, no honest Christian can deny that the main business left to New Testament Christians by the Saviour in the Great Commission is to win souls.

In the parable of the man who made a great supper and

bade many, in Luke 14:16-24, we are told that the servant went first to those who had been invited. They would not come. Then he was to go into the streets and lanes of the city, and invite "the poor, and the maimed, and the halt, and the blind." Then he was to go into the highways and hedges of the country, and urgently, compellingly persuade them to come! Does not that indicate that the Lord Jesus holds the Christians of a local congregation accountable for everybody within possible reach of the Gospel?

A similar parable is Matthew 22:1-14, where the king commanded his servants, "Go ye therefore into the highways, and as many as ye shall find, bid to the marriage." The servants "went out into the highways, and gathered together all as many as they found, both bad and good: and the wedding was furnished with guests." That is the scope of soul winning responsibility of the Christians in every local church.

II. New Testament Christians and Churches, Our Examples, Won Multitudes Continually

The young church in Jerusalem took literally those commands and followed that program. In Acts 5:42 we are told, "And daily in the temple, and in every house, they ceased not to teach and preach Jesus Christ." Their activity was so great that within a few weeks, the high priest and the council had Peter and John arrested saying, "Did not we straitly command you that ye should not teach in this name? and, behold, ye have filled Jerusalem with your doctrine, and intend to bring this man's blood upon us" (Acts 5:28).

Paul the apostle reminded the elders of the church at Ephesus of this responsibility to reach every person with the Gospel in soul-winning entreaty and witness. He reminded them that he had for three years not shunned to declare the whole counsel of God "...I kept back nothing that was profitable unto you, but have shewed you, and have taught you publickly, and from house to house, Testifying both to the

Jews, and also to the Greeks, repentance toward God, and faith toward our Lord Jesus Christ" (Acts 20:20, 21). Again, giving them the example of what they should do and what their membership should do and what other Christians should do, he said, "Therefore watch, and remember, that by the space of three years I ceased not to warn every one night and day with tears" (vs. 31). This Bible standard of total witnessing, saturation effort to win souls, is very clearly the Bible standard for churches which represent Jesus Christ on earth.

Now let us see how the Christians in early churches won multitudes of souls. Consider the church at Jerusalem, at Pentecost and after. Acts 2:41 tells that after the preaching of Peter at Pentecost, "Then they that gladly received his word were baptized: and the same day there were added unto them about three thousand souls." The Christians earnestly tried to win everybody, and here we have three thousand people joining the converts and being baptized in one day.

In Acts, chapter 3, Peter and John healed a lame man at the Temple, then preached to the people and persecution began. But Acts 4:4 says, "Howbeit many of them which heard the word believed; and the number of the men was about five thousand." First, there were about three thousand added to that little group of 120. Now they have so multiplied that the men alone, besides the women and children and young people in the churches, were about five thousand! No wonder, for Acts 2:47 had said, "...And the Lord added to the church daily such as should be saved." They were having many people saved daily, and the church grew into a multitude, with about five thousand men.

Acts 4:32 speaks of this group at Jerusalem thus: "And the multitude of them that believed were of one heart and one soul." Now they had passed counting by the thousand. Those who believed and trusted Christ are now a "multitude."

After the judgment of God on Ananias and Sapphira, we are told in Acts 5:14, "And believers were the more added to the Lord, multitudes both of men and women." Acts 6:1 tells us, "And in those days, when the number of the disciples was multiplied, there arose a murmuring of the Grecians against the Hebrews, because their widows were neglected in the daily ministration." The number of disciples were not only "added," as at Pentecost, but now "multiplied." Later, following the death of Herod in Acts 12:24, we are told, "But the word of God grew and multiplied."

Pentecost was a specimen day, ushering in a period of time which Joel 2:28-32 calls "the last days," which will go on until the "great and notable day of the Lord," as Peter quoted it in Acts 2:14-21. So the growth of the church at Jerusalem is set up as a model for Christians who have set out to take the Gospel to all the world.

In Samaria, where Deacon Philip went to preach, we are told in Acts 8:6, "And the people with one accord gave heed unto those things which Philip spake, hearing and seeing the miracles which he did." Again in verse 12, "But when they believed Philip preaching the things concerning the kingdom of God, and the name of Jesus Christ, they were baptized, both men and women." Such a wonderful tide of the power of God and people being saved was normal for New Testament churches.

In fact, Acts 9:31 says, "Then had the churches rest throughout all Judaea and Galilee and Samaria, and were edified; and walking in the fear of the Lord, and in the comfort of the Holy Ghost, were multiplied."

The churches were "multiplied," that is, the converts were multiplied and the churches grew. That was a regular, consistent pattern of these New Testament churches where Christians set out to win everybody they could and witnessed daily.

III. Despite Persecution, Amid Heathen, Blinded People, They Won Multitudes

Those who were persecuted in Jerusalem were scattered abroad "as far as Phenice, and Cyprus, and Antioch" (Acts 11:19). Verse 21 says, "And the hand of the Lord was with them: and a great number believed, and turned unto the Lord." "A great number" of those who heard believed and turned to the Lord. Barnabas came to Antioch, a Spirit-filled man, "and much people was added unto the Lord" (vs. 24).

Paul and Barnabas, on a missionary journey, came to Iconium "into the synagogue of the Jews, and so spake, that a great multitude both of the Jews and also of the Greeks believed" (Acts 14:1). Christians in New Testament churches won multitudes of souls and that on mission fields where we would think conditions are most severe.

At Thessalonica Paul and Silas came to preach and Acts 17:4 tells us: "And some of them believed, and consorted with Paul and Silas; and of the devout Greeks a great multitude, and of the chief women not a few."

Then Paul and Silas went to Berea and we read in verse 12 of Acts 17, "Therefore many of them believed; also of honourable women which were Greeks, and of men, not a few." Those are the terms that described the soul winning in New Testament churches. "Many of them believed," and "of men, not a few."

Paul went to Corinth and there the same fine, exultant note reports the results of the new church. "And Crispus, the chief ruler of the synagogue, believed on the Lord with all his house; and many of the Corinthians hearing believed, and were baptized" (Acts 18:8). Paul stayed there eighteen months, for God had told him, "I have much people in this city" (Acts 18:10). A tremendous church of believers was assembled in that short time.

At Ephesus a similar, remarkable ingathering of souls was on the young church where Paul preached, as we see from Acts 19:18-20: "And many that believed came, and confessed, and shewed their deeds. Many of them also which used curious arts brought their books together, and burned them before all men: and they counted the price of them, and found it fifty thousand pieces of silver. So mightily grew the word of God and prevailed."

The terms reporting converts in New Testament churches are in "thousands" when they were counted, or "many," or "not a few," or "multitudes."

The amazing growth of New Testament churches is almost beyond our comprehension. Warnock, in his History of Protestant Missions, says that at the end of the first century, six or seven years after Pentecost, there were about 200,000 Christians. He says that by the end of the third century there were 800,000 Christians despite vigorous persecution and martyrdom of thousands. They were now one-fifteenth part of the Roman Empire! And these converts were won among Jews, the same kind of blinded Jews who crucified the Lord Jesus Himself, and among heathen people, idolaters, and that, despite bloody persecutions throughout the Roman Empire. Despite the martyrdom of Stephen and James at Jerusalem and many others, persecuted "unto the death, binding and delivering into prisons both men and women" (Acts 22:4), and the imprisonment and attempted murder of Paul, thousands were won among the Jews. Despite the bloody persecutions of Nero, who had Paul and many others beheaded; the persecution under Hadrian and particularly under Antoninus Pius, Marcus Aurelius and Septimius Severus, still the blazing fire of evangelism went on. Workman says:

> For two hundred years, to become a Christian meant the great renunciation, the joining a despised and persecuted sect, the swimming against the tide of popular prejudice, the coming under the ban of the empire, and the possibility at any moment of imprisonment and death

under its most fearful forms. For two hundred years he that would follow Christ must count the cost, and be prepared to pay the same with his liberty and life. For two hundred years the mere profession of Christianity was itself a crime.

Under Emperor Valerian the persecution was very severe and the official Roman Empire persecution came to an end in A. D. 313 under Constantine. In the midst of the most adverse circumstances, violent hatred, persecution and "closed doors," New Testament Christians carried on their amazing soul-winning work.

How does the soul winning of our churches compare with New Testament teaching and practice?

2. Our Churches Generally Fail to Win Souls

When we compare the amazing growth of the New Testament churches in the first three centuries, under the worst persecution and opposition, we find a startling contrast in the work of American churches and Christians today. Compared to the New Testament churches and New Testament Christians, our present-day churches and Christian people generally fail disastrously and shamefully.

I. Unconverted Liberals, Deniers of the Historic Christian Faith, Do Not Win Souls

First, we must write off the cults which do not preach the Gospel of salvation by personal faith in Christ. Those who do not believe in the deity of Christ, His blood atonement, and in the new birth by regeneration, by personally trusting Christ as Saviour, do not win souls. The Unitarians, Christian Scientists, Christadelphians and Mormons, for example, cannot be counted as winning souls in the New Testament fashion.

We must, of course, write off the modernists, the liberals, who do not believe that the Scriptures are the authentic, authoritative and infallible Word of God; who do not believe in the deity, virgin birth, bodily resurrection and blood atonement of Jesus Christ; who do not believe that people are by nature sinful and lost and must be born again by faith in Christ. Such liberals do not win souls. They do not claim to get people converted, to get people to personally know Christ as Saviour in the sense that New Testament and historic Christianity does.

II. Liturgical Churches Do Not Win Many Souls

Also, we will need to leave out of our consideration a great many of the liturgical churches. There are fundamental, Bible-believing groups in Lutheran, Episcopal and Reformed churches who preach the Gospel and win souls, but it is sadly true that in most liturgical churches confirmation takes the place of conversion. One godly man, a great preacher, pastor of one of the largest churches of his denomination, prominent in denominational councils, begged me to come for a second revival campaign in his church. He said that half of his official board were unsaved and that hundreds of others of his church members were unconverted, having been taken into the church through catechism classes and confirmation. If that was so under the sound Bible preaching of that man, a far worse state would be found in the liturgical churches where they know only form, memorized prayers, and no evangelistic preaching or teaching.

I think we would be compelled to say that most of the liturgical churches are not winning souls. Some among them are converted, but the soul-winning emphasis and soul-winning results are usually negligible in such churches. Individuals such as Bishop Ryle of Liverpool, Bishop Taylor Smith of England, Dr. William Culberson, Episcopalian and Dr. Walter Maier, Lutheran, are exceptions in soul-winning emphasis.

But in the most evangelistic and orthodox of denominations, the number of souls won is small. Some years ago I set out to have a strong interdenominational committee select the ten best soul-winning churches in America to be rated on membership, Sunday school attendance, and the number of converts baptized in a year. I was shocked to discover that not a single Methodist, Presbyterian, United Brethren, Disciples, or Assembly of God church, or any of other faiths could be compared in evangelistic impact and results to some Baptist churches. And since Baptists regularly take no unaccountable infants into membership and no one else without a public profession of faith in Christ, the baptisms in Baptist churches would usually be something of a measure of the soul-winning success of a church.

III. Consider Soul Winning Among Southern Baptists

The largest evangelical group of Protestants in America is the Southern Baptist denomination. The 1962 Annual lists 32,892 Southern Baptist churches with a total of ten million members, averaging 309 in members per church. But these churches won an average of 11.6 converts baptized per church per year. In other words, it took 27.7 members a year to win one convert and get him baptized!

On the foreign mission field Southern Baptists had 35,509 converts baptized, with 2,078 missionaries on the field. However, there were 3,783 organized churches on the mission field, 6,850 chapels, a total of 10,633 churches and chapels, most of them with national pastors and with nearly a half million members on the field. So, while there were about 17 baptisms per missionary per year, that was only 3 1/3 baptisms per church or chapel won by the missionaries and national pastors and the half million church members together.

Southern Baptists are the most evangelistic of all larger denominations in America, and it took each 27.7 members a year to win a convert and get him baptized!

I am informed that last year, of the thirty-two thousand plus Southern Baptist churches, some six thousand did not baptize a single convert, and some six hundred such Baptist churches in my State of Tennessee baptized not a single convert in the year!

It is shockingly and tragically true that our churches do not win souls in any way comparable to the record of New Testament churches.

IV. Consider the General Association of Regular Baptist Churches

In their most recent report for the year ending April, 1964, they had 1,156 churches, with a total membership of 158,689. They reported 8,198 baptisms. That was one baptism to 19.4 members. That is, it would take one member 19.4 years to win a soul, or that many members one year to win a soul and get him baptized. That was slightly more than seven baptisms per church among these General Association of Regular Baptists.

V. The Christian and Missionary Alliance Report on Soul Winning

The general secretary of the Christian and Missionary Alliance, Dr. W. F. Smalley, kindly sent me the annual report of the home department (as distinguished from their very strong foreign mission work) for 1964. It was prepared by the home secretary, Rev. L. W. Pippert, who says:

> A recent study reveals that among the Evangelical Protestant churches of the nation, less than 10 reported 300 or more conversions a year, and less than 20 congregations reported up to 200 conversions.
>
> Both in the Alliance and without, a substantial percentage of churches cannot report a single accession in the year. No one can take issue with the position that something is radically wrong spiritually, when churches lean upon institutional techniques, hoping to do by organization and tradition that which basically is the responsibility of the witnessing believer.

The report shows 1,235 Christian and Missionary Alliance churches, including 21 new churches with a total membership of 73,629 and with 3,248 converts baptized in the year. Since the average membership was less than 60, that averages 2.6 converts baptized per church and one convert was baptized for each 22 1/2 members. It took 22 1/2 people a year to win a soul.

VI. Presbyterians Report Only 1½ Additions Per Church for a Year

In the 1964 meeting of United Presbyterian men in Chicago, it was reported that "the 9,500 congregations of the United Presbyterian churches in the United States had a membership gain of only 1 1/2 persons last year." Since membership in a Presbyterian church does not necessarily involve conversion, then we could not say that Presbyterian churches had 14,250 conversions last year simply because they had that many additions. At very best no Bible-believing Presbyterian would say that Presbyterian churches are winning many souls to Christ.

In fact, Dr. George Sweazey, former head of the Presbyterian Evangelism Commission, speaking at the meeting, said that the church is "but one generation from extinction and is daily under attack from the cemeteries and from the maternity hospitals."

In Columbus, Ohio, May, 1965, the 3,300,000 group reported that it took 317 Presbyterians to add one member, not necessarily saved, in a year!

VII. Canadian Independent Baptists

My associate, Dr. Jack Hyles, was some months ago in an annual meeting of Bible-believing and fundamental Baptists in Canada, and he brought back the sad report that the churches had averaged 5 1/2 baptisms per church per year in the preceding year!

Now when one remembers that among liberal churches, and liturgical churches, and Pedobaptist churches which "baptize" infants, and, which receive members without requiring evidence or even profession of personal conversion, personal saving faith, it is obvious that even church additions are not all converts. Even the best, most orthodox churches win relatively few souls compared to the millions left unsaved, and compared to the New Testament standard and practice.

Sadly we must say our churches do not win many souls!

VIII. There Are Blessed Exceptions: Some Churches Do Win Many Souls

It is obvious that in giving the statistics for any great group of churches, those who win no souls are somewhat covered in the averages, and churches that do win many souls are robbed of their credit. In the denominational groups which do not win many souls per church or per hundred members, there are some churches that win many, as well as some that win none.

But in spite of the fact that in these modern days the worldliness, the sinful course of society, and the indifference among Christians that all fundamental, Bible-believing churches face, some churches do win souls. That proves it can be done.

Consider the great Temple Baptist Church in Detroit where Dr. G. Beauchamp Vick is the pastor. That church some twenty-five years ago, before the ministry of Dr. Vick, had a few hundred in Sunday school each Sunday, baptized a few dozen converts each year. Now with the tidal wave of personal soul winning and week-by-week evangelism, with no letup, that church has grown to be perhaps the largest church in the world, with thousands of members, and the Sunday school often runs between 4,500 and 5,000 per Sunday. A recent inquiry brought out the fact that in the preceding year there had been over 1,400 converts received as candidates for baptism in that church, and that was about the usual annual number of converts for baptism.

What Temple Baptist Church can do in a great northern metropolis like Detroit, other churches in similar circumstances can do.

Consider the Highland Park Baptist Church of Chattanooga where Dr. Lee Roberson is the pastor. That church has grown from a modest suburban church with a few hundred members, with an auditorium seating only six hundred, to one of the largest churches in the world. For fifteen consecutive years the pastor has baptized over 1,000 converts

per year! The last church year the number of converts baptized was 1,358, and this soul winning goes on day after
day, week after week, despite the tremendous missionary
outreach with about 160 missionaries, with the Tennessee
Temple Bible College, Institute, and Seminary, and with a
ministry in many other churches where the pastor goes for
one or two days between Sundays. And that is in a southern
city crowded with churches, particularly Baptist churches.

About five years ago Dr. Jack Hyles was called to pastor
the First Baptist Church of Hammond, Indiana. It was a
rather typical downtown, formal, rich, and rather worldly
First Baptist Church. There were millionaires in the
church. The former pastor was president of the ministerial
association, one former pastor had gone to the secretary-
ship of the Indiana Baptist Convention (American Baptist),
one had gone to the presidency of Gordon College at Boston.
The pastor preached in formal clothes; the services were
formal.

Under the Spirit-filled ministry of Dr. Hyles, there came
a spiritual revolution in the church. Some of the wealthy
worldlings left. The entire church was reorganized. Formal services were made informal, evangelistic. Soul winners were trained and put in all places of leadership. Last
year in that church there was an average of approximately
30 professions of faith per Sunday, with over 1,000 converts
baptized, and the attendance in a few years has grown from
less than 1,000 to a recent average attendance of 2,200 and
a top attendance of 3,450 (not on Easter).

Hammond is a Chicago suburb, is in the midst of the steel
district, a typical northern city with a large foreign element, predominantly Catholic. If the First Baptist Church
of Hammond, Indiana, can win souls in that fashion, then
other churches in similar situations throughout the Chicago,
New York, Philadelphia, Baltimore and St. Louis area can
do the same.

The blessed success of some churches and some groups

of Christians in winning souls proves that it can be done. The causes of failure should be sought, found and rooted out.

We thank God that many Bible Baptist churches and other independent Baptist churches are specially strong in house-to-house soul winning and in continuous evangelism, trying to reach every individual in their communities for Christ, and often with amazing and happy success.

But most churches win few souls.

3. Most Church Programs Minimize Soul Winning

We suppose that all born-again Christians who really love the Lord Jesus would like for our churches to win more souls. Most Christians would not want the church to be fanatical about it; they would not want to be thought fools and extremists by the outside world, and they do not want a real revolution in the program of the church. They would like for the church to win more souls on the plan that they already have, in ways that would not embarrass anybody, would not lose any members, and would not make compelling demands on the members.

But the simple fact is that most churches do not win many souls because they are not set up to win souls. Soul winning is practically ignored or is minimized in the plans and organization and program of the average church, even the churches where the Gospel is preached and where people generally believe the fundamentals of the Christian faith. Such churches believe in soul winning, but they minimize it and do not organize all the program of the church to this one major end.

But there is no half-hearted, easy way to win a multitude of souls, and there is no way to have a great soul-winning church without sacrifice, without a drastic revolution in the organizational aims, programs, plans and administration of the church.

Back of our fruitlessness in the churches is the simple fact which we should honestly face: our churches are not set up primarily as soul-winning agencies. Our program, our plans, our emphasis is not that of the great New Testament soul-winning churches, though certainly their great soul-winning program ought to be ours.

Before we give details in which the church minimizes soul winning, will you consider the testimony of a tremendously successful soul-winning pastor.

Dr. Mark Matthews, long pastor of the First Presbyterian Church, Seattle, with whom were associated six ministerial assistants, twenty-eight Sunday schools, and who held the office of Moderator of the General Assembly, once gave the following answer to the question: "How do you fill your church?"

First--This church has been filled for nearly eleven years. Most of the time it is crowded, and scores and hundreds have been turned away. The evening audiences number anywhere from 2,500 to 3,500. We can only seat about 3,000. The rest have to stand or be crowded out. The audience has in it from 55 to 70 per cent of men. The church is doing an immense amount of work. Frequently there are from six to eight services running at the same hour in the different rooms of the church.

Second--The results accomplished are entirely due to the operations of the Holy Spirit. We pray much, expect much and get much.

Third--The pure, simple gospel is preached. Sinai and Calvary are held up to the people. The vicarious atonement is emphasized; the sacrifice of Christ is presented daily; His deity and His mediatorial work are kept before the people. The whole gospel, and nothing but the gospel, is preached.

Fourth--We make the gospel apply to every condition, circumstance, and point of a man's life. We deal with his social, domestic, commercial, political, civic life, with the gospel and only the gospel.

Fifth--Every service is an evangelistic service. We never preach the gospel or finish a sermon without making an appeal for immediate decisions and confessions of Christ. At every service we urge men to accept Christ

and join the church. In other words, we try to demon-
strate a passion for souls with profound love for God,
implicit confidence, faith and trust in Christ and in leadership of the Holy Spirit.

Sixth--We do not have a sermonette after a long musical programme of questionable ecclesiastical music.
Every member of the choir must be a Christian and
spiritual music must be used, but that programme is
kept in its minor place. The sermons are not dictated by
the clock, nor are they closed at the suggestion of some
man who would like to hurry through the service. Time
enough is taken to present the case of sin, produce conviction in the hearer's mind and ask for the work of the
Holy Spirit to produce conversions. In other words, we
all work, and we all work at the business of saving souls,
preaching the gospel and believing absolutely the promises of Jesus Christ.

A study of the program and work of most of our present-
day churches, even Bible-believing churches, shows that
soul winning is minimized, played down.

I. Pastors Usually Called to Serve the Membership, Not Primarily to Win Souls

Some years ago I was invited to be present and offer
counsel in an official church board meeting which was to
recommend the calling of a pastor. The church had over six
hundred members and almost without exception they were
Bible-believing Christians, generally clean in their lives,
liberal in their giving, faithful in attendance. The church
was in a college town. It had many teachers from a Christian college and from a Bible institute in the membership.
This church was so generous in its giving that they gave a
large part of the support to forty foreign missionaries.

As they discussed a certain man whom the officers wanted
to recommend as pastor, one man stood up and said, "Is he
a soul winner? Have you learned how many converts he has

seen baptized in his present pastorate? Does his record indicate that he could help us build a great soul-winning church here?"

An older member of the board said with a smile, "Young brother, we are not so much interested in numbers here. What we want is Bible preaching and let God take care of the results."

But the wise young brother answered, "I understand that the church is not too much interested in numbers. From the records, I see that this church baptized only four converts, all little children, in the last year!"

They wanted a pastor to preach the Word, to teach them, to marry their children, bury their dead, comfort them when they were sick, and give them an enjoyable church program. They were not primarily interested in having a pastor lead in soul winning.

In 1932 I was led to have a blessed independent revival campaign in Dallas, Texas, and out of this grew the large Galilean Baptist Church. I remained as pastor for seven and a half years. We had by God's great mercy a multitude saved. In one six-month period we had a count of 1,005 people who claimed the Lord as Saviour, including some backslidden Christians who returned from their wayward, open sin, renewed their vows and started out again in a happy Christian life. Probably only one-third had ever professed faith.

Inevitably, the calls were so many for my soul-winning ministry that I was away from this church several weeks in each year, although God continued to bless the local church. The good people bought me a new car, then some pleaded with me, "Brother Rice, don't take the car out of town. We want you here to come to visit us when we are sick, and to marry our young people, and to comfort us in trouble, and bury our dead." But I told them that I must put first things first. Jesus said, "What man of you, having an hundred sheep, if he lose one of them, doth not leave the ninety and nine in the wilderness, and go after that which is lost, until he find it?" (Luke 15:4).

The very term "pastor" has come to mean looking after Christians, and pastors who win few souls or none say that they are called to "feed the sheep." And the churches are glad to think that they are God's sheep and that the pastor ought to spend his time in feeding them, teaching them the Word of God and otherwise making himself useful to church members.

The average pastor's work includes not only preaching Sunday morning, Sunday night, and conducting a midweek service; it goes all the way from taking his car to pick up ladies who want a ride to the missionary society or to the washeteria, drinking tea or punch in the ladies' meeting, trying to be a good fellow in the Rotary or Lions Club, counseling a husband and wife who are about to have a divorce, and trying to keep their son from going to the reformatory.

It is true that the Lord Jesus said to Peter, "Feed my lambs" and twice, "Feed my sheep" in John 21:15, 16, 17. And Peter did just that, too, when he preached at Pentecost and along with the testimony of many others, he saw some three thousand people claim the Lord and follow Him in baptism! The Lord Jesus meant "the lost sheep of the house of Israel" (Matt. 10:6) when He said, "my sheep." So the Lord told Ezekiel, "My sheep wandered through all the mountains, and upon every high hill: yea, my flock was scattered upon all the face of the earth, and none did search or seek after them" (Ezek. 34:6). He spoke of the dispersed nation Israel.

In the parable of the lost sheep the lost sheep was as much His sheep as were the safe ninety and nine. And Jesus told the woman of Canaan that He was "sent...unto the lost sheep of the house of Israel" (Matt. 15:24). Often the Lord Jesus looked on the poor lost multitude and had compassion on them for "they were as sheep not having a shepherd" (Mark 6:34)! So the principal duty of every preacher is to seek first the lost one, even if he has to leave the ninety and nine in the wilderness.

In Ephesians 4:11 and 12 the Lord tells about the work of preachers, whether they be apostles, prophets, evangelists or teachers. "And he gave some, apostles; and some, prophets; and some, evangelists; and some, pastors and teachers; For the perfecting of the saints, for the work of the ministry, for the edifying of the body of Christ." But follow on through the six verses, 11 to 16, because there is no period and the sentence does not end until the 16th verse.

So the preacher's work is to "perfect the saints for the work of the ministry," so that the "whole body...maketh increase of the body...." The pastor is to teach people to win souls and so increase the body of Christ. Dr. Jack Hyles says here, "Until a church is organized right it cannot reap right."

II. "Missions" Put As a Substitute for Soul Winning in Local Community

"Missions" is a magic word. Foreign missionaries in other days made such sacrifices and won such victories that the hearts of good people everywhere go out to one who is truly a missionary. So denominational leaders began calling the whole denominational program "missions." If money is needed to build a seminary, or a hospital, or to pay the big salaries of secretaries, it is called "missions!" You see, people give better to missions than to some other things.

But churches, too, have fallen into a sinful self-deception here. Again and again I have heard pastors say that the blessing of God on the church would depend on how much they gave to missions! And yet, the same man might do little to win souls himself or to lead his church locally in soul winning! I mentioned above a church that had forty foreign missionaries, yet had only four people claim Christ as Saviour in a year's time.

Such churches have altogether ignored the order which the Lord Himself gave: "But ye shall receive power, after that the Holy Ghost is come upon you: and ye shall be witnesses unto me both in Jerusalem, and in all Judaea, and in Samaria, and unto the uttermost part of the earth" (Acts 1:8). Jerusalem first, then Judaea, then Samaria, then the uttermost part of the earth. No church is doing right which does not put the immediate responsibility for your local community ahead of all other responsibilities as far as soul winning is concerned.

The Lord told His disciples that "repentance and remission of sins should be preached in his name among all nations, BEGINNING AT JERUSALEM" (Luke 24:47). Yes, to please God every church must begin at its own Jerusalem.

That great church at Jerusalem sent no foreign missionaries and were not commanded to do so until they won many thousands in Jerusalem. Then when great persecution came, they were driven out and they went winning souls wherever they could. They understood, and we ought to understand, that Jesus meant that their first great soul-winning responsibility was in their own town and area.

I have been on the mission fields in India, Korea, Japan, and I found a sad and shocking truth: The missionaries who go out from churches which do not win souls, do not win many souls on the foreign field. The foreign mission field comes last in God's plan about soul winning and not first, according to the Great Commission. If that be heresy, then go look at the Great Commission again and make the most of it!

The best soul-winning churches are great foreign mission churches, too, but do not make that an excuse for disobedience in local soul winning.

III. Those Who Set Standards for Churches Do Not Make Soul Winning First

The seminaries and Bible colleges which train Christian

workers do not set up the standard that ministers of God are primarily to be soul winners and that the program of a church is to be soul winning, daily, weekly, all the time, and before everything else.

The best Bible colleges and the sound Bible-believing seminaries generally teach Bible. They teach Hebrew and Greek. They teach homiletics and related subjects. Some of the best have courses in personal soul winning. But I do not know more than two or three which teach would-be pastors that soul winning is a major program of the church. They are taught to have formal worship services. In the best of them they are taught expository preaching. But they are not taught how to have revivals, how to give an invitation, how to build a strong soul-winning visitation program, how to win hundreds through the Sunday school.

One pastor who had attended the then best-known independent Christian college in America and the best-known independent fundamental theological seminary, a man with a doctor's degree and pastor of a large church, told me woefully, "They taught me to load the gun, but they never told me how to shoot it!" He knew much Bible, but not how to win souls.

In a principal Ohio city, a young Episcopal minister came to me in deep concern. He was assistant in a large Episcopal cathedral. The rector was about to resign and he would be advanced to the principal responsibility as pastor. This young man was a graduate of a principal college, with an A. B. degree. He had then graduated from Yale Divinity School. Sadly he said to me, "I was taught how to balance a teacup on my knees, and to chat with the ladies. I know how to tell a good joke and meet with the Rotary Club. But if a drunkard wanted me to tell him how to be saved, I would not know how to begin! How can I take the rector's place in this great church when I don't know how to win souls!"

Even in the training of missionaries, it is shocking how little people are taught about soul winning. A leading representative of one of the major faith missions said to me one time, "Dr. Rice, why don't you support a foreign missionary?"

I replied, "I have long wanted to do that. If I knew a man worthy of support, one who is trying to do on the mission field what I am trying to do at home, I would support him personally."

He replied, "I have just the man for you! He has already been accepted by our mission board and is ready to go. I will bring him to see you."

So the young man came to see me. He was a graduate of a well-known Bible institute. Yes, he was sound on the fundamentals of the faith, as I soon discovered. He believed the Bible. He was willing to sacrifice and go to the foreign mission field to spend his life.

"Now, how many souls have you won to Christ?" I asked him.

"Well, I think I ought to get credit for helping to win some," was his reply. "I sang with a quartet for two summers on the field for the Bible institute, and in two of those services people were converted. I think I ought to have part of the credit for people being saved in those two services."

I was chagrined. Here was a man who had already finished his training, had been accepted by a mission board, was going to Africa, and he had never personally won one soul to Christ! How could I use God's money to pay his way to the foreign mission field?

A good many publishing houses get out a pastor's manual each year. They have suggestions for Christmas, Palm Sunday, Ash Wednesday, Good Friday, Easter; suggestions for Mother's Day, Father's Day, Memorial Day and Thanksgiving. They have seed thoughts, talks to children; they have jokes to tell. These books teach preachers to be occupied with routine administrative matters and keeping church people happy, with very, very little emphasis on soul winning.

The denominational magazines say much about the denominational program, say much about the schools, the hospitals, about civil rights, about retirement, about tithing, and
boost the annual meetings, but they are not calculated to
help pastors put soul winning first in the church. The pro-
fessors who train ministers are usually not themselves soul
winners. They generally criticize evangelists and evangelistic preaching. They mock at any special fervor about
preaching or about tears or holy enthusiasm.

Those who set standards for pastors and churches do not
put soul winning as a major emphasis.

IV. Often Those We Might Win Are Planned Out of the Services!

Did they have any city rescue mission in Jerusalem in the
book of Acts? No, the church itself was a rescue mission!
"And daily in the temple, and in every house, they ceased
not to teach and preach Jesus Christ." But now, we have left
the skid-row bums, the ragged poor, those in the cults, and
those guilty of the grosser sins, outside the plans of the
church. The churches have gone out of the rescue mission
business.

The very poor are not encouraged to attend most churches. If the church does not go out into the highways and
hedges and compel them to come, they will not come. We
should remember that Jesus said, "The Spirit of the Lord is
upon me, because he hath anointed me to preach the gospel
to the poor..." (Luke 4:18). A church that is not set up
primarily for the poor is not set up for the biggest crowd;
therefore does not put soul winning first.

A fervent, Spirit-filled pastor whom I know went to an old
downtown First Baptist Church, formal, rich, cultured. He
enlisted scores and scores of people to take part in house-
to-house visitation. They worked up bus routes to bring in
to the services hundreds of children and young people from
far and near. Some were poorly dressed, some were dirty,
some did not know how to fit into the routine of a big city

church, but they were loved and hundreds of them were won to Christ.

A wealthy member approached the pastor indignantly. "What are we going to do with all these dirty-nosed children here?"

The pastor answered, "I don't know what you are going to do about them, but I am going to love them with all my heart."

The wealthy man replied sternly, "If they stay, I go!"

So they stayed and he went. The church that appeals mainly to the rich will not have many to win. The church that leaves out the poor, the ill-dressed, the ignorant, the drunkards, the harlots and the bums, will not have the main crowd it ought to be winning to Christ. Don't write off Jehovah's Witnesses and Christian Scientists and Catholics and other cults! The church should seek to win "every creature" and should "go out into the highways and hedges, and compel them to come in" (Luke 14:23).

Many years ago I was in two weeks of revival services in a church in Akron, Ohio. The church was old, not very large, but we had good advertising and a good deal of visitation, and as I recall there were nearly one hundred professions of faith. Many of these and others applied for church membership and baptism. Near the close of the second week I was invited to speak at a woman's missionary meeting after their extended program. I arrived in time for my message, found two big rooms of the home crowded with women, and all about the place were parked Cadillac and Packard cars. I was taken in through the kitchen because the front of the house was so crowded. There I saw food prepared by a caterer that must have cost thirty or forty dollars--refreshments for this ladies' meeting. When I was brought into the group, I was surprised to find that most of the faces were strange. These people had not been attending the revival services. I found there was a good deal of complaint about the revival. These prosperous women and their husbands were saying, "That man is getting the church full of poor people! And if the tire factories close down in the winter, we will have to feed the whole bunch!" When I rose to speak, I asked how long it had been since that "missionary society" had seen anybody saved. Nobody answered. So I began at one point in the great circle and insisted that each particular person tell me if he remembered anybody who had ever been won to Christ in that meeting or by the women of that meeting! Pitilessly I pressed the matter around the circle. One woman had known of somebody won to Christ privately some years before. None of them had ever known of anybody saved through the women's meeting itself.

I shamed them and told them they should disband and form a Bible class, with the pastor in charge, to teach them how to win souls and lead them in soul winning. Immediately one woman made a motion they disband and organize such a class. The vote was carried almost unanimously. However, I am sure that the whole pattern of a church is not changed that suddenly. And that church declined and finally disbanded. I am only illustrating that our churches are not set up to win souls.

In Sherman, Texas, in our big open-air revival campaign on the courthouse lawn, a poor drunkard and dope addict heard me one night, became deeply convicted and came to see me the next day, wanting to know if such a sinner as he could be saved. "I didn't sit on the seats," he told me, "because I knew that if I was there nice people wouldn't come and sit near me. I sat on a pile of stones away in the back where I could hear." I was surprised at his opinion, but I found that he knew people's attitude toward outrageous sinners better than I did. He was converted, a few people rejoiced, but many criticized, and many said, "He won't hold out."

In 1925, when I was pastor of the First Baptist Church, Shamrock, Texas, a woman of bad reputation was converted.

Her joy, her humility, her devotion to Christ were beautiful to see. She joined the church and I had the honor to baptize her. Then I insisted that she join the ladies' Bible class in the Sunday school and attend the women's missionary meetings. Promptly she answered, "I should like to attend, but I think the women wouldn't want me."

"Oh, yes," I insisted, "they will be glad to have you. They will expect you to come." To encourage the matter, I spoke to a fine Christian woman who taught the large class of women in the Bible school and was a leader of the missionary society. I suggested that she should encourage the new convert, the woman who was baptized last Sunday night, to attend the class and the missionary meeting and feel at home with the women of the church.

To my astonishment this good woman replied, "I do not think that is the thing to do. That woman has a very bad reputation and I fear it will hurt our standing in the community if such women as that attend our Sunday school class and women's meetings."

I do not mind saying that I boiled over. I said, "That woman is coming to that Sunday school class of women and to the missionary meeting. She was truly converted. She loves the Lord. Her past is behind her. I do not know anything about her except that her reputation is not good, but now that is forgiven and forgotten. If I learn that you or any woman in this church withdraws from this new convert, embarrasses her, makes her feel ill at ease and unwelcome, God helping me I will publicly, from the pulpit, brand the woman who does it as the hypocrite she is! I will not be pastor of a church that will not welcome any poor, fallen woman who repents of her sin and comes to Christ."

Churches that develop bus routes and have someone calling from house to house far and near, planning to pick up the children or all who will come at a certain set promised time on Sunday morning, find they can have a multitude of children and young people and many of the very poor in the

services week after week. In the First Baptist Church of
Hammond, Indiana, some 750 are brought every Sunday by
buses on routes that are carefully planned and carefully de-
veloped with hundreds and hundreds of calls week after
week. So it is with the Highland Park Baptist Church, Chattanooga. But the church where a man cannot feel at home
without a tie, without a new suit, is not going to see many
souls won.

Often our churches have a "junior church." The regular
auditorium services are so stiff and formal and cold that
little children do not understand, do not appreciate it, so
these children are sent to the basement where a young
woman teaches them how to have a formal church service.
Thus they are away from the parents and they cannot dis-
turb the dignity of the cold, dead church upstairs! But most
of the converts in any church ought to be those in the Sunday
school or those who are enlisted by Sunday school workers.

I have found by taking careful check in cities all over A-
merica that the average born-again Christian found Christ
before he was fifteen years old. Anybody who reaches the
age of fifteen and is not saved has already lost over half of
his opportunities to ever be saved in America. Oh, we had
better make the preaching and the singing such that the
children can understand and be blessed and so that they can
hear it and be saved. I think there is a place for a baby
nursery. Mothers and others will hear better when little
babies, crib babies, can be left in a nursery and are carefully cared for by loving hands, while Mother and Dad attend
the preaching of the Gospel. But a mother will sometimes
come with a number of children who will not stay in the
nursery, and if she cannot come with her children, she will
not come at all.

V. It Would Take a Revolution to Adjust the Program of Most Churches to Put Soul Winning in Its Rightful, Pre-eminent Place

How can a church major on soul winning and pursue that

blessed task with holy abandon when the official board is made up of cold, unspiritual, and even sometimes unsaved men? In the Bible, the requirements for the deacons at Jerusalem were, "Look ye out among you seven men of honest report, full of the Holy Ghost and wisdom, whom we may appoint over this business" (Acts 6:3). And among them was Spirit-filled Stephen who preached with such mighty power and was the first Christian martyr. Among them was Philip who was such a great soul winner that he turned out to be an evangelist and held great revivals in Samaria and elsewhere. Church officials ought to be fervent, Spirit-filled soul winners.

Most pastors feel that if they can have the cashier of the bank on the official board, or a prominent judge, or newspaper editor, or the superintendent of schools, they will get more money and the church affairs will be handled in a more "businesslike way." Often the purpose is prestige, as well as money. But how can such men contribute soul-winning emphasis when they themselves never win souls and are not sold on soul winning and when they are primarily anxious to please the worldly members and outsiders?

No, it will take a revolution to make the average church into a mighty soul-winning organism.

The pastor ought to teach the people bit by bit the standards the New Testament holds up for leadership in the church. Every deacon, every trustee, every Sunday school teacher ought to be selected by the church and pastor on the basis of personal soul winning and helping to make the church into a soul-winning church.

It would mean revamping the choir and the music program of the church. It would mean leaving off some of the most popular kind of preaching for the kind that cuts, burns, convicts and saves. It would mean offending many worldly members, perhaps driving some of them from the church and getting others converted. The basic program, planning and administration of the average church is so far from the

New Testament standards that it cannot win souls without a revolution within the church to make it into a soul-winning church in passion and power and in all-consuming zeal.

4. Most Pastors Do Not Personally Win Souls

One reason why our churches win so few souls is that the pastors themselves win so few. There is much truth in the proverb, "Like people, like priest." In the next chapter we will study how the preaching often fails to win souls, fails to stir people to win souls. But now we speak not of the preaching in the pulpit but of the personal soul-winning efforts of the pastor himself. A pastor who does not personally win souls will not make soul winners out of others. One who does not practice soul winning will not preach soul winning very effectively. And the man who does not have burden enough and power enough to win souls personally, will not have the burden and power he needs in the pulpit. The pastors themselves ought to be mighty soul winners.

I. Pastors in Personal Work Alone Could Win Far More Souls Than They and All Their Congregation Now Win

Yes, I mean just that. The average pastor, by giving a few hours a week to most earnest work, seeking and having the power of God upon him, as any ordinary Christian can have, could win far more souls than he and his entire congregation now win in a year's time. The failure in our churches is, first of all, a pastor failure. There is no way to build great soul-winning churches without soul-winning pastors. And here is the first and easiest key to building soul-winning churches. Let the pastor himself become a faithful soul winner, honestly setting apart a certain number of hours every week to seek the lost and win them, and get them into the services to claim Christ openly.

For example, in Southern Baptist churches averaging 309 members per church, there was an average of only 11.6

converts baptized in a year. So if a pastor himself won one person every month, he would win as many in a year's time as the average Southern Baptist church wins in a year's time with all its services, its preaching and revival efforts! Do you really believe that any fervent, Spirit-filled pastor who sets aside time to pray, then time to actually seek out lost people, could not win more than one soul a month or twelve souls in a year's time?

The General Association of Regular Baptist churches, smaller in size, won on the average slightly more than seven converts to be baptized in a year for each church! Does any serious, earnest Christian believe that a Spirit-filled pastor could not win more than seven souls himself, alone, a year if he worked at it with fervent heart and along with earnest prayer?

Those Canadian churches that averaged 5 1/2 baptisms per year--could not the pastors of these churches, if they gave themselves earnestly to personal soul winning, win more than 5 1/2 souls each per year?

Recently my son-in-law, Billy Carl Rice, left an assistant pastorate in Portsmouth, Ohio, to go to another large church in Kalamazoo, Michigan. Dr. Otis Holmes, the pastor of Temple Baptist Church in Portsmouth, published a commendation of the departing assistant pastor, saying that in two years' time he had won over 500 people to Christ! In one week, in Portsmouth, Ohio, he won seven souls; four of them were past fifty years old. In Kalamazoo, Michigan, I know that in one recent week Billy Carl won eleven.

On June 25, 1933, I had been pastor of a church ten months, now the Galilean Baptist Church. On that night I asked the people to agree with me to try to win a thousand souls by Christmas, just six months away. I urged those who would to earnestly wait on God and set a quota as to how many he felt God would help him win in that time. We knew one godly woman who that week had won five to Christ. My wife, greatly burdened, said that she would earnestly try to win fifty; another fervent and godly woman undertook to win thirty in the six months. A seamstress, Mrs. Hardesty, said that if Mrs. Rice, with five daughters, a large Sunday school class, and with the duties of a pastor's wife could win fifty, then she ought to win a hundred. In the six months' time, Mrs. Rice won a few more than one hundred souls to Christ. Mrs. Hardesty won more than 150! In the next year she won 360! And most of these were adults, and some were hardened sinners. Of the 1,005 people who were won to Christ in that six months' time, most of them were won by very ordinary Christians who had only high school or grade school education, no Bible institute or seminary training.

I found that personal soul winning does not require necessarily the gifts and the education that may be needed in the pulpit. Many a pastor who is only an ordinary preacher can be a tremendous soul winner. There was Hillus Gass in Dallas, a most ordinary and commonplace kind of young man. He was saved and I baptized him. He got a burden on his heart to win souls, so he began to work at it. He went to the Texas Centennial World's Fair at Dallas to do personal soul-winning work among the crowds there. After watching him carefully and checking on his work for some time, I bought him a season ticket, and that summer he and a companion who worked with him day after day brought me names and addresses of over 500 people who had claimed Christ as Saviour.

Pastors like to think that the amazing results of over 30 professions of faith per Sunday at First Baptist Church, Hammond, are won by great preaching or by great organization. All that helps, but of the thousand or so baptized the first year of Pastor Jack Hyles' ministry there, 250 were won by the pastor personally in house-to-house visitation, and 190 more were won by Assistant Pastor Jim Lyons. All the staff must win souls, and report weekly.

Now let me say it again: if the pastors of our country

should themselves put personal soul winning in the prominent place God gives it, and actually spend time and effort, along with their earnest prayer, they could win more souls personally than they and all their congregations now win in a year's time. Most of them could win ten times as many!

II. "Call to Preach" Primarily Means Personal Soul Winning

Many preachers personally win very few souls because they think of themselves as men called of God to preach. They have in mind particularly the public services, the sermons preached to crowds. On that matter I believe we have misunderstood and have perverted what preachers are commanded to do. As a preacher I must say that I am called to preach. But actually I am called to win souls, whether by ones or twos or hundreds or thousands, but primarily dealing with individuals as individuals.

Is not that the clear meaning of the Great Commission as given in Mark 16:15, 16, where we are commanded: "Go ye into all the world, and preach the gospel to every creature. He that believeth and is baptized shall be saved; but he that believeth not shall be damned." Is the command that we are to "go and preach the gospel," to every congregation, every organized church? No, indeed it is not. The Great Commission call to preach is, "Preach the gospel to every creature," that is, to every individual. The Christian who talks to one man about the Lord, gives him the Gospel, urges him to be saved, is preaching in the clear sense of the Great Commission. And the primary purpose of God's call is that we shall win souls.

Do not misunderstand me. I believe that God has called me to preach in the sense that He wants me to give my whole life to getting out the Gospel. I know that that involves speaking in public to crowds, preaching sometimes over a great radio network to perhaps millions and perhaps preaching the Gospel through THE SWORD OF THE LORD to perhaps 80,000 homes and more, and to the millions who have read some twenty-four million copies of my books and pamphlets around the world in thirty languages. But I know that the immediate and first meaning of the Great Commission in Mark 16:15, 16 is that I am to go to individuals and that individuals who trust in Christ are saved, and those who do not trust Him are lost. The Great Commission more definitely commands personal soul winning than public preaching to congregations. Churches may hire preachers to preach, but God calls a preacher to win souls. And he is as much in the will of God, and is even more clearly and literally following the command of the Lord Jesus in the Great Commission, when he goes out and seeks people and wins them.

Isn't that the meaning of the parable of Jesus, concerning a man who made a great supper and bade many and sent his servant to knock on doors and "say to them that were bidden, Come; for all things are now ready" (Luke 14:17)? Isn't that what Jesus means when He tells of the master commanding the servant, "Go out quickly into the streets and lanes of the city, and bring in hither the poor, and the maimed, and the halt, and the blind" (vs. 21)? Isn't that the meaning of the command to "go out into the highways and hedges, and compel them to come in, that my house may be filled" (vs. 23)? Surely the inference of the parable is that soul winning is primarily by an individual going after individuals.

Is not that the way Jesus did it Himself? We know that He preached to great multitudes, but we do not know that usually people were saved while He preached to the crowds. He won Nicodemus one night alone. He won the woman of Sychar in Samaria at the site of Jacob's well. He won blind Bartimaeus by the roadside near Jericho, and Zacchaeus up a sycamore tree beside the path! He won the woman who was a sinner at the house of Simon the leper; the woman taken in adultery as she stood shamed and broken before Him. Jesus, the Master Preacher, continually won souls personally. Is not He the proper pattern for us as preachers?

And is not that the pattern of the New Testament churches? Is not that the way New Testament churches principally won souls? We see Peter and John win a lame man in the Temple when he was healed. We see Philip win the Ethiopian eunuch, and Paul win Sergius Paulus in spite of the distraction of Elymas the sorcerer. And of the New Testament Christians it is said, "And daily in the temple, and in every house, they ceased not to teach and preach Jesus Christ" (Acts 5:42). Surely God intended the preacher's first concern to be soul winning, and that his principal activity about soul winning should be person to person.

There is a wonderful place for evangelistic preaching, but a preacher can win souls when he cannot get lost people to attend the church services, when he cannot publicly answer their questions and problems. The hospitals are full, many with sad and troubled people with time on their hands and with fear of death and with heart tendered by God's dealing. The jails are full of people disillusioned, troubled and with time on their hands. Any preacher by spending an hour perhaps at a bus station or at a washeteria or courthouse or supermarket, can find many lost people to whom he can speak about salvation. In the families of every church are lost people whom the preacher could seek out. Many of them he could win.

Oh, the call to preach is a call to win souls, and perhaps the preacher is called even more to win souls personally and privately, than publicly and professionally.

III. Many Preachers Do Not Know How to Win Souls or Know Little About It

In a county-wide Baptist association meeting in Texas, I spoke on personal soul winning. Then a pastor of the largest church in the county, a First Baptist Church (Southern Baptist) rose and said, "I believe that the brother is right. Surely he is! But I do not know that I have ever personally won a soul to Christ. I have had a few people saved under my preaching and they came forward to claim the Saviour, but I never did sit down with the Bible to win a lost soul. I would not know how to go about it." That man believed the Bible. He was a born-again man, a good man. His hair was gray. Now after being pastor for many years of the largest church in the county, he told his brethren sadly that he had never personally won a soul to Christ!

When I was assistant pastor of the First Baptist Church of Plainview, Texas, we arranged for a nationally known Baptist evangelist to come to Plainview and prepared for extended services in the city auditorium. He was a good preacher and a good many were saved. One night I talked to a drunkard for whom prayers had long been made. He was soon in tears. Yes, he saw now he was a wicked sinner, enslaved by habit. He needed the Saviour.

I thought that it would be a blessing for the evangelist to deal personally with this drunkard, and so in the midst of the invitation I went and whispered to him, "Here is a drunkard for whom many have prayed. Now he is ready to be saved. Would you like to deal with him personally?"

He was embarrassed and said to me, "No, Brother John, I would not know what to say. You deal with him or take him to my father." He preached a good gospel message but he did not know how to win a drunkard!

I preached in a city-wide campaign at Lewistown, Pennsylvania, some years ago. When the meeting began to break and many people began to claim Christ as Saviour, I had arranged for the pastors in the inquiry room to deal carefully with every person who came forward. But the Presbyterian pastor, a Bible-believing Christian, graduate of Princeton University and Princeton Seminary, said to me, "What can I do? I do not know how to win a soul to Christ in the inquiry room. I do not know how to answer their questions. What can I do?"

I had him stand by me and when a sinner came to trust

Christ and take my hand, I would ask him clearly if he was now ready to turn from his sins and depend on Jesus Christ as Saviour. When there was a definite "yes," I would let this Presbyterian pastor take the convert by the hand and lead him to the inquiry room for one of the other pastors to deal with more thoroughly, then this pastor would come back to stand by me again. It was sad that here was a trained preacher who believed the Bible, but who had never personally won a soul.

I am sure that one reason why many pastors win so few souls is that they do not know how. The matter is not clear in their own minds how to bring a sinner to see himself as lost and how to make clear the plan of salvation and how to bring one to a decision. But how can pastors who do not clearly see how to win a soul, teach their members how to win a soul and have a great soul-winning church?

It has been a great privilege of mine to know many of the best soul-winning pastors in America, and these men are not necessarily the greatest preachers. Their success is that they win souls and teach others to win souls.

Dr. Lee Roberson is pastor of the Highland Park Baptist Church at Chattanooga, Tennessee, with the many, many duties of a pastor of thousands of members and with a number of full-time assistants in the church. He is also the president of Tennessee Temple Schools. Dr. Roberson has a number of radio programs during the week. Regularly he goes to other preaching engagements, at least two days a week. His church supports about 160 foreign missionaries. He plans never to be away from his church on Sunday morning, or Sunday night, or Wednesday night. When we were discussing personal soul winning, I asked Dr. Roberson about how much personal visitation and soul-winning effort he found time to do. He answered, "I try to make ten calls a day when I am in town." If Dr. Roberson can look for ten lost people a day and try to win them, so can pastors with lesser responsibilities.

I know well Dr. Jack Hyles, pastor of the First Baptist Church of Hammond, Indiana. I know that he has carefully and rigorously set aside certain hours every week in which he visits prospects and goes from house to house, aside from lost people he finds in the hospital wards when visiting his own church people.

A pastor who does not personally win souls cannot teach nor inspire others to win souls. And he will find he has, usually, little evangelistic fire in his preaching.

5. Preaching in Most Churches Does Not Build Soul-Winning Membership Nor Win Many Souls

When on their missionary journey, Paul and Barnabas came to Iconium and went into the synagogue of the Jews, they "so spake, that a great multitude both of the Jews and also of the Greeks believed" (Acts 14:1). Not only the content of the message but the manner and spirit in which they spoke led a multitude of sinners to repent and trust in Christ for salvation.

We are told of the powerful preaching of Peter at Pentecost in Acts, chapter 2, verse 37: "Now when they heard this, they were pricked in their heart, and said unto Peter and to the rest of the apostles, Men and brethren, what shall we do?" Spirit-filled, scriptural preaching has a major part in turning men to Christ. A hot pulpit makes a warm church. So Spirit-filled preaching is essential to making a soul-winning church.

It is true that more people are won to Christ by personal contact than by hearing a sermon without personal contact and witness. But it is also true that the right kind of preaching builds soul winners, brings conviction, arouses the conscience and makes a climate for soul winning, in addition to teaching people how to win souls and stirring them to this solemn duty commanded by Jesus Christ of every Christian. One cannot well put personal soul winning as against the public evangelistic services, since they are largely interdependent. No church wins many souls without the kind of preaching that makes soul winners and attracts lost people and brings them out to claim Christ as Saviour.

But we think it is a sad fact that most churches do not have the kind of preaching that attracts lost people and convicts the unconverted, that trains and inspires personal soul winning. Because of the lack of evangelistic preaching, Sunday school teachers do not make the Sunday school itself an evangelistic hotbed. The church officers are more concerned with records and buildings than with soul winning. The choir is more occupied with aesthetic and formal music than with soul winning. The preacher himself by his preaching must set the standards, create the climate and spur soul-winning efforts. Sadly, most churches do not have that kind of preaching!

I. Pastors Usually Do Not Have the Convictions, Faith and Boldness to Preach, Teach and Live As Prophets of God

In those glorious days of the New Testament when the Gospel spread like wildfire and multitudes were saved, God's preachers were made of stern stuff. Jesus had solemnly warned His disciples that to be His disciples meant taking up the cross and the way of crucifixion; that the servant was no better than his Lord and the world that hated Jesus and crucified Him would hate true witnesses also. They expected abuse, opposition, misrepresentation, beatings, imprisonment, and sometimes death. And they paid that price gladly. The Bible shows a clear connection between that boldness and persecution and the soul-winning power they had.

In Acts 5:17-42 we find Peter and John arrested, tried before the Sanhedrin, and only the intercession of Gamaliel kept them from following out the plans they had made when they "took counsel to slay them." They were not killed; but listen now to these verses that follow:

> "And to him they agreed: and when they had called the apostles, and beaten them, they commanded that they should not speak in the name of Jesus, and let them go. And they departed from the presence of the council, re-

joicing that they were counted worthy to suffer shame for
his name. And daily in the temple, and in every house,
they ceased not to teach and preach Jesus Christ."--
Acts 5:40-42.

Beaten for preaching the Gospel so plainly, as they had
already been imprisoned in the same chapter, now they went
out from that beating "rejoicing that they were counted worthy to suffer shame for his name!" Then followed the natural and inevitable result: "And daily in the temple, and in
every house, they ceased not to teach and preach Jesus
Christ."
See the boldness of Stephen before the Sanhedrin and Jewish leaders, openly charging them with the murder of Jesus!

"Ye stiffnecked and uncircumcised in heart and ears,
ye do always resist the Holy Ghost: as your fathers did,
so do ye. Which of the prophets have not your fathers
persecuted? and they have slain them which shewed before of the coming of the Just One; of whom ye have been
now the betrayers and murderers."--Acts 7:51, 52.

How boldly did Peter preach at Pentecost! "Jesus of Nazareth...ye have taken, and by wicked hands have crucified
and slain," he said in Acts 2:22, 23. Again in the next sermon Peter said to them, "But ye denied the Holy One and the
Just, and desired a murderer to be granted unto you; And
killed the Prince of life, whom God hath raised from the
dead; whereof we are witnesses" (Acts 3:14, 15). See the
boldness and decisive action of Peter in facing Ananias and
Sapphira with their lying to God and his boldness in an-
nouncing that God would slay them, as He did.
See Paul, facing Elymas the sorcerer who hindered the
conversion of Sergius Paulus. "Then Saul, (who also is
called Paul,) filled with the Holy Ghost, set his eyes on him,
And said, O full of all subtility and all mischief, thou child
of the devil, thou enemy of all righteousness, wilt thou not

cease to pervert the right ways of the Lord? And now, behold, the hand of the Lord is upon thee, and thou shalt be blind, not seeing the sun for a season" (Acts 13:9-11).

Oh, you timid preachers, afraid of deacons and rich and worldly members, I beg you, see Paul standing before Felix so that that wicked governor trembled, before Agrippa and Festus, and again and again before the Jewish leaders who hated him! There are too many boys in the pulpit where we need men; too many men-pleasers when we need God-pleasers; too many loyal denominationalists when we need loyal prophets.

In Bible times there were no official boards to run the business of the churches. The word deacon is an English transliteration of the Greek word which means servant. The apostles at Jerusalem told the people, "Look ye out among you seven men of honest report, full of the Holy Ghost and wisdom, whom we may appoint over this business" (Acts 6:3). They were servants of the churches, to work under the direction of the preachers. There is not a hint in the Bible that a group of businessmen, deacons, or elders ought to call the preacher, or control the preacher, or control the financial affairs of a church, or accept or reject members. The pastor should be God's man and he should so manifestly be God's man and have God's power that he can influence and lead the church.

That means that many churches need a revolution before they can become great soul-winning churches.

Too often the pastor is counted only as a hired man. He has no authority in the Sunday school nor over the Sunday school teachers, no authority over the teachers, no control of the choir and the church music, no control of church property, building and grounds. Worldlings in the church count him as a grasshopper and like the spies which went into Canaan, he often is only a grasshopper in his own eyes.

In one church I know, which was professedly fundamental and orthodox, the deacons gave orders to the pastor that he was not to have a public invitation to accept Christ in the services any more. In another great city church, generally fundamental but rich and worldly, when they called a new pastor, already a church committee had signed up visiting choirs, representatives of colleges, seminaries, and mission boards to fill over fifty of the regular services in a year's time! When the assistant pastor put up in his office in the church a picture of his wife and children, he found it taken down with a note that that would have to be approved by the building and grounds committee.

Frequently when a Spirit-filled preacher takes a strong stand against worldliness and for an evangelistic program in the church, influential and rich laymen withhold financial support or bring pressure to bear through denominational headquarters.

So preachers often do not have the conviction, faith and boldness to grow great soul-winning churches.

There was a time when a minister was called "preacher"; now he is called "the minister" or "Reverend." In the Sunday school, once it was urged that people "stay for preaching"; now they are urged to "stay for church." Preaching is minimized because the preacher himself does not have the boldness, power and spiritual leadership preachers once had.

II. Evangelism, the First Duty of Every Pastor

The first aim of every preacher called of God should be to win souls. A minister may say, as an alibi for his powerlessness and fruitlessness: "I am called to be a teaching pastor. My ministry is to the church. I must feed the flock of God." But that, I insist, is an alibi for outright disobedience to the plain command of God. The Great Commission is still binding on preachers. The Gospel is to be preached to every creature. We are to teach those already converted to go win others.

It was to Timothy, as the pastor of a great church in Eph-

esus, that Paul wrote, "Do the work of an evangelist" (II
Tim. 4:5). R. A. Torrey was a pastor, but what a soul
winner! Charles H. Spurgeon was a pastor all his days and
never called himself an evangelist. Yet multiplied thousands were saved under his ministry, and the Metropolitan
Tabernacle was called a "soul trap." The Apostle Paul himself would pass very well for a Bible teacher! How he taught
the young Christians, appointed and trained elders in every
church, is a marvel. His fourteen epistles are the deepest,
richest doctrinal teaching in the Bible. Yet Paul regularly
did the work of an evangelist and had more to do than all
other apostles did, with the evangelizing of the whole Roman
Empire in his lifetime!

In America all the great pastors have been great soul
winners. Consider Jonathan Edwards, T. DeWitt Talmage,
A. B. Simpson, George W. Truett, R. G. Lee, W. B. Riley,
Oswald J. Smith, H. A. Ironside, P. W. Philpot, Louis T.
Talbot, J. C. Massey. Remember that D. L. Moody, J.
Wilbur Chapman, R. A. Torrey and other leading evangelists were for long years pastors. So pastors can be, and
all true pastors will be, soul winners. The pastor who is
not a soul winner is a backslider, a disobedient Christian,
proving untrue to his holy vows and to his divine calling.

The tendency in churches all over America is that pastors
shall give their principal attention to the church members.
Calling, visiting the sick, the hospitals, marriages, funerals, church finances, denominational business, the choir,
young people's meetings, the women's societies--these
things occupy the time, interest and labors of the average
pastor, largely to the exclusion of soul winning. That is
utterly foreign to the New Testament practice and teaching.

The Saviour said, "What man of you, having an hundred
sheep, if he lose one of them, doth not leave the ninety and
nine in the wilderness, and go after that which is lost until
he find it?" (Luke 15:4). God's plan is that every under-
shepherd should have the same interest and pattern in his

ministry as the Great Shepherd, the Lord Jesus, had. He said the normal thing is that a shepherd (pastor means shepherd) should leave the ninety-nine sheep who are not lost, even if they are out in the wilderness instead of in the fold, and go after the one sheep which is lost.

Oh, if a preacher would learn to "leave the ninety and nine in the wilderness and go after that which is lost, until he find it"! And the Saviour said, in justification for this teaching, that "I say unto you, that likewise joy shall be in heaven over one sinner that repenteth, more than over ninety and nine just persons, which need no repentance." A pastor ought to be more concerned over one soul that is lost, than over ninety-nine church members who are saved! A pastor's preaching ought to be largely addressed to the unconverted.

That will mean that part of his preaching will be in the jails, or on street corners, or in country schoolhouses, or to groups of children or young people in private homes, or to service clubs, or in tent campaigns. But the preaching in the church services ought to be strongly evangelistic, as well as the preaching in other places. One principal reason why our churches do not win souls is that the ministers of the churches so rarely preach to unconverted people.

III. There Is Usually Little Preaching to Set the Soul-Winning Standards

A church cannot be filled with worldly people, and especially cannot be controlled by worldly people, and have many souls saved. Often such worldly people are entrenched. They have kin people in the church. If the preaching is plain, they may withhold gifts, they may oppose the pastor's leadership. But what can the preacher do if the Sunday school teachers themselves attend movies, use tobacco, serve cocktails, keep beer in the icebox, take the young people on mixed swimming parties, act as chaperons at high school dances? What if champagne or cocktails are served at the wedding reception of the deacon's daughter? What if a prominent member owns a building rented for the sale of liquor?

Some churches try to solve the difficulty simply by passing certain rules or making certain requirements in the church constitution that Sunday school teachers and officers or church officers must meet certain standards. But that is not enough. Unless the sentiment of the whole church is actively aroused and enlisted, such rules become dead letters. The thing must be settled by the right kind of preaching, building sentiment. It must be plain preaching but it must be Spirit-filled preaching that will win the support of born-again Christians. The preaching may cause a revolution in the church. It may and probably will lose members. It may lead to a demand for the pastor's resignation; the preacher may suffer for it.

But where can we find an argument that Bible Christians were not to suffer for Christ and that pastors today are not to be willing to have some hardship, some misunderstanding, some reproach for being true to Christ? Better that the pastor have to move and start over elsewhere, for being true to Christ, than to go on giving his consent to a dead and powerless church, thus prostituting his ministry by tacit approval of or consent to flesh-pleasing standards that dishonor Christ and make a great soul-winning program impossible!

Usually the preacher can win, if the power of God is on him. And if he cannot win one place, he can win in another, provided he is still in the will of God and preaches the Word of God with power.

We are saying that preaching must make a climate where God can save souls or the preacher must accept responsibility for a church that is largely powerless and fruitless. If the preaching does not lead Christians to godly living, it cannot lead them to be soul winners. Then Christians need preaching on soul winning. Sunday school teachers, church officers ought to be continually reminded that according to Acts 6:3 they are to be "full of the Holy Ghost and wisdom" and, like Stephen and Philip, they are to be active soul winners. Workers need challenge and instruction. I well know from long experience that red-hot preaching, combined with constant example on the part of the pastor, can raise up many spiritually minded, consecrated, active soul winners in a church.

Our churches win few souls partly because preachers do not continually set Bible standards of separation, consecration, spiritual power and soul-winning activity for the people.

IV. Too Often Preaching Does Not Make a Strong Issue Over the Fundamentals

Years ago my revered friend, the late Dr. James M. Gray, president of Moody Bible Institute, said editorially in Moody Monthly that perhaps preachers ought to specialize, that some ought to be Bible teachers and not try to be evangelistic, some ought to defend the faith, and some ought to be evangelists and soul winners. But in my humble judgment, that noble good man was wrong. The great themes of the depravity of the human heart, the atoning death of Christ, the need for the new birth, salvation by grace through faith, a literal Heaven and a literal Hell, are evangelistic themes. And they necessarily involve the deity of Christ, the virgin birth, the bodily resurrection, and they are the fundamentals of the Christian faith.

The pastor who does not expect to win many souls can preach nice little sermons on civil rights, on the United Nations, on the community chest, on brotherly love. But the man who expects to arouse the conscience, stir the emotions and bring the will to a holy repentance and decision, must preach on great truths of the Bible.

It is no accident that the great soul winners have been defenders of the faith. Spurgeon carried on a noble campaign against "the Downgrade Movement," now called modernism, and left the Baptist Union of Great Britain and Ireland at a great cost of reproach, and led that great church out, because of the sin. And Spurgeon's preaching wonderfully upholds the inspiration and authority of the Bible, the deity of Christ, and all the other fundamentals of the Christian faith.

R. A. Torrey was a great Bible teacher and a defender of the faith, as well as a world evangelist.

It is surprising perhaps to one who has not studied them to find in the sermons of Billy Sunday a strong defense and teaching concerning all the fundamentals of the Christian faith, including the Second Coming.

The best soul-winning pastors have often been great Bible teachers and defenders of the Christian faith. Among them are W. B. Riley, mentioned above, who built the largest church in all the North while he was president of the World's Fundamental Association; Dr. T. T. Shields of the Jarvis Street Baptist Church in Toronto; Dr. John Roach Straton of famous Calvary Baptist Church in New York City. And Dr. J. Frank Norris of the First Baptist Church of Fort Worth, while not the example we would choose in some matters, yet proved that a strong defense of the faith fitted properly with the building of a great evangelistic downtown church with hundreds of converts baptized each year.

Once in Dallas, Texas, Dr. Mordecai Ham, a mightily used evangelist, and I, were in conversation about the fight then on among Texas Baptists about the verbal inspiration of the Bible. I had some small part in that defense of the faith, and eventually the state secretary and other principal leaders in Texas came out openly for verbal inspiration of the Bible. But Dr. Ham told how one prominent pastor had said to him, "What does it matter whether or not the Bible is inspired word for word in the original manuscripts? We know it is in some sense the Word of God."

Dr. Ham told me that he replied: "It may not matter to you. Some of you pastors go on with a regular program in your well-organized churches, and if God should die, you might go on a year before you found it out! But as an evangelist, if I am to convert drunkards, harlots, infidels and gray-headed sinners, I must preach a Bible that is absolutely and infallibly the Word of God, and I must preach it with a holy boldness that comes from that certainty."

It was my privilege to found and to be for seven and a half years pastor of the Galilean Baptist Church in Dallas, Texas, which grew to some 1700 members in that time, baptizing frequently over 300 converts a year, while I made an open issue in an attack on modernism, on the theory of evolution, and as we taught in detail the great fundamentals of the Christian faith.

As long as there is doubt in the mind of the preacher or in the minds of his hearers as to the absolute authority of the Bible as the infallible Word of God, his message is weakened, the impact on the community is watered down, the reasons for soul winning are diminished.

It is no accident that the greatest soul-winning churches in America are fundamentalist in position, out and out for the great truths of the historic Christian faith, including even the premillennial coming of Christ. So with Highland Park Baptist Church in Chattanooga; First Baptist Church in Hammond, Indiana; Temple Baptist Church, Detroit; High Street Baptist Church, Springfield, Missouri; Baptist Temple of Akron, Ohio; Baptist Temple of Canton, Ohio; First Baptist Church of Dallas, Texas; Beaver Street Baptist Church of Jacksonville, Florida; Trinity Baptist Church of Jacksonville, Florida; and many, many more. I dare say that of the twenty or more churches in America that baptize two hundred or more converts a year, the pastor in every case takes a plain, sharp stand for the fundamentals of the Christian faith, all announce themselves as fundamentalists, all are premillennial.

V. Expository Preaching, Without Arranging Scriptures to Bring a Definite Result, Fails to Win Souls

At the risk of being misunderstood, I must say that expository preaching, as it is usually done in Bible-believing pulpits, does not grow soul-winning churches. I know that the pastorate is required to be "apt to teach" (I Tim. 3:2), and that God's people ought to be taught the Word of God. But unfortunately most expository preaching is more or less a routine matter, is not aimed at particular objects. It may help in some Christian graces and in general soundness of the faith, but it does not make soul winners.

I do not excuse those shallow preachers who take a verse of Scripture as a pretext and preach a topical sermon without preaching what the Scripture itself means or without expounding the Word of God. It is commanded that a preacher should "preach the word," as Paul told Timothy.

But it is important to note that of all the sermons mentioned in the Bible, none were expository sermons with one possible exception, as far as I know. That one exception is in Nehemiah 8:8 where Ezra the scribe, with certain helpers, stood on a pulpit of wood and "read in the book in the law." "And he read therein before the street that was before the water gate from the morning until midday, before the men and the women, and those that could understand; and the ears of all the people were attentive unto the book of the law" (Neh. 8:3). And it is said again of Ezra and his helpers, "So they read in the book in the law of God distinctly, and gave the sense, and caused them to understand the reading" (vs. 8).

I think they read with comments, but it was not what we would call an expository sermon. And no sermon that Jesus preached, neither the Sermon on the Mount, nor in His many parables, did He ever preach what is now called an expository sermon. And so with the sermons in the book of Acts by Peter, by Stephen and by Paul--none were expository sermons. In every Bible case a preacher stood up to preach to get a certain result, and he preached toward that result. So ought preachers today preach toward a certain end, not simply to expound the Bible Itself for Its own sake. Preachers love to say, "We gather around the Word." But we should remember that "the letter kiileth," even the letter of the Word of God, if It be not preached with power and with direct intent and application by the Spirit.

I have the forty-volume set, The Bible of the Expositor and the Evangelist, sermons by the late Dr. W. B. Riley, preaching through the Bible in the latter years of his long ministry in the First Baptist Church of Minneapolis. I am also aware that that beloved good man had fewer conversions in the later years of his life when these sermons were preached. Although he often had the evangelistic services on Sunday evening, to bind himself to a plan of preaching on through the Bible without any particular reference to whether it should bear on the immediate needs of the people or bring them to conviction and repentance, greatly limited the soul-winning results in his ministry, in my judgment.

I am familiar also with the volumes of Addresses by the late Dr. H. A. Ironside, my good friend who for years gave sermons to THE SWORD OF THE LORD, of which I am the editor. Because there was a demand for his Bible teaching, he would frequently go Sunday after Sunday preaching through a certain book of the Bible whether or not it had any relation to the immediate needs of the people or to winning souls. Although there were usually one or two or three and sometimes five public professions on Sunday, other men who have much less congregations than the 3,500 or 4,000 who often heard Dr. Ironside in that giant Moody Church in Chicago, have far more conversions. I know several such churches that regularly have from fifteen to fifty public professions of faith every Sunday. But it is not through expository preaching, following a set course simply to teach the Bible.

Every fishing line should have a hook to catch a fish.

Preachers should be "fishers of men." Every whip should have a cracker on it. Every dose of medicine should be prescribed to bring a particular result. Every sermon preached should have a definite aim and should be followed by an urgent demand for action. To "gather around the Word" as if one were in a museum examining an ancient sword, as if it were a sword stained in ancient times with blood, nicked in many a conflict but now exhibited for the gaze of the curious, is not a proper use of God's Word, and does not tend to build soul-winning churches.

The preaching of the great soul winners has been Bible preaching in some sense, but never expository preaching. No other pastor perhaps has preached to so many people and had so many conversions as did Charles H. Spurgeon. His sermons were expositions of a text, usually one verse, sometimes two, and were filled with allusions and references to the Scriptures, but they were not expository sermons.

So with the preaching of R. A. Torrey, D. L. Moody, J. Wilbur Chapman, Charles G. Finney, Sam Jones, A. C. Dixon, P. W. Philpot, Bob Shuler, John Brown, Bob Jones, Sr., Paul Rader. The sermons that get people saved, the sermons that make soul winners are usually not expository preaching, following the usual pattern of going through a book chapter by chapter or section by section.

In my own evangelistic messages, I try to make sure that the sermon is an honest interpretation of the text, and I strive to prove and enforce and illustrate every point in the sermon with Scriptures. Writing an ad on one of my books of twelve sermons, a worker found there was an average of thirty-eight different Scriptures quoted per sermon. Preaching ought to be Bible preaching, but evangelistic, and the kind that builds evangelistic churches must be preaching toward a particular need, to get definite results, not simply routine exposition of some Scripture that may have no immediate, urgent application to a Christian to win souls, or to a lost sinner to repent and trust Christ for salvation.

VI. Scholarly, Cultured, Quiet Preaching Misses the Multitude

It takes a certain kind of preaching to get people saved. A man may preach the Gospel and preach it correctly and actually preach it to sinners, yet never get anybody saved.

The preaching must be of the type that will attract attention, will get crowds, will cause deep interest. God wants the man on the street, and the preacher should preach to him. God wants the housewife, the high school student, the child. What a sin for the preacher not to want them and not to preach so as to attract them to the services and get their interest, their consciences, their decision for Christ! Some preachers aim their sermons at the cultured, the learned, the well-taught. That is a fatal mistake that has ruined many a preacher's ministry. Oh, human pride! Oh, the fear of men! Oh, worldly ambition that longs for reputation as a scholar! These are not for the pastor who expects to win souls.

Do not think that D. L. Moody won souls in spite of his simplicity. Rather he won souls because of his simplicity. Do not think that Billy Sunday won souls in spite of his slang, his commonplace expressions, his acrobatics on the platform, his plainness of speech. Rather he won souls because of these things. God is interested in common people, ignorant people, sinning people, and Billy Sunday was interested in the same crowd and worked to save them.

Preachers, then, ought to preach on great controversial subjects, subjects in the minds of common people. There should be sermons on Hell, on judgment, on the second coming of Christ (I do not mean a dry, abstract teaching of minute details concerning prophecy). He should preach on adultery, on drunkenness, preach on the Bible and the present war, on death, on divorce. This kind of preaching, plain Bible preaching, controversial preaching, proving each point by the Word of God, helps to get crowds. Crowds came to hear Moody, just as they came to hear Billy Sunday, just as they came to hear Wesley and Whitefield and Spurgeon and

Torrey, whether they agreed with them or not. Bold, uncompromising, controversial preaching; preaching that condemns sin, that fights heresy, that shows the way out of trouble, that warns people of the wrath of God, such preaching gets crowds. It will attract unsaved people as well as the saved.

People went to hear Aimee Semple McPherson preach, and they did not go because they like heresy better than truth. Rather they went because they were interested, they were intrigued, they were moved. As long as "Christian Science," Spiritism, Seventh-Day Adventism and Pentecostalism get crowds, we could get them if we worked at it as they do.

VII. Preaching Often Does Not Win Souls Nor Build Soul Winners Because It Does Not Bring Strong Condemnation Against Sin

Some preaching does not show what God says about the wickedness of particular sins and the inevitable punishment that comes for sin. Such preaching has no holy indignation; it does not burn the conscience; it does not make the sinner fear Hell and judgment; it does not make Christians aware of the awful doom of the Christ-rejecting sinner.

Those who think more of pleasing people than of pleasing God, more of keeping peace than of promotion of Bible preaching, often scorn preaching against sin as "negative preaching." But when God in nine of the Ten Commandments says, "Thou shalt not," the preacher has good reason to preach, "Thou shalt not." There is more in the Bible about law than there is about grace. The Bible puts repentance before faith. So the preacher who bypasses God's plan and preaches faith without preaching repentance, preaches grace without preaching law, will find that he has ignored the divine plan and so missed the divine blessing.

Some who are psychologically minded more than Bible minded scorn the fear motive. But the Bible says that Noah, "moved with fear, prepared an ark to the saving of his house" (Heb. 11:7). Noah, properly scared, did right, and he and his family were saved. That was better than dying in the flood. And it is better for a man to be frightened when he learns about the ruin that sin brings, and the Hell that awaits the Christ rejecter, and so turn from sin to trust Christ. The preacher who does not preach as Paul did to Felix on "righteousness, temperance, and judgment to come," will not have hearers tremble as Felix trembled! Preachers who do not openly, boldly accuse Christ rejecters of their wicked rejection of Christ, will not have hearers "pricked in their heart" and "cut to the heart" as Peter did and as Stephen did (Acts 2:37 and Acts 7:54).

This wicked, modern idea that parents are not to whip children, that the state should abolish the death penalty, that preachers should not preach on Hell, is satanic and contrary to Bible Christianity.

Paul commanded Timothy, "Preach the word; be instant in season, out of season; reprove, rebuke, exhort with all longsuffering and doctrine" (II Tim. 4:2). He was inspired to tell Titus, "For there are many unruly and vain talkers and deceivers, specially they of the circumcision: Whose mouths must be stopped, who subvert whole houses, teaching things which they ought not, for filthy lucre's sake. One of themselves, even a prophet of their own, said, The Cretians are always liars, evil beasts, slow bellies. This witness is true. Wherefore rebuke them sharply, that they may be sound in the faith" (Titus 1:10-13). The preacher who does not "rebuke them sharply" does not have Christians sound in the faith nor sinners seeking the Lord.

The command in Isaiah 58:1 is: "Cry aloud, spare not, lift up thy voice like a trumpet, and shew my people their transgression, and the house of Jacob their sins." God has not changed, nor man, nor sin, nor the mercy of God since that command. A preacher cannot get Bible results without the Bible kind of preaching, with the Bible emphasis on sin and judgment. People who do not know they are sick, do not go to the doctor. Sinners who do not know they are sinners, do not repent.

The fervent denunciation of sin, showing by the Bible its wickedness, promising mercy to those who repent, has some wonderful effects greatly to be desired.

First, it helps get crowds to hear the Gospel. The sad fact is that in many of our churches lost people, the general public, do not attend because there is nothing especially pertinent and applicable to their lives in what they see and hear. The infidel would not be warned. The drunkard would not see pictured the tragedy of his enslavement and the way to freedom from his bondage. The harlot would not be made conscious of her filth, nor see the way to be cleansed and become pure in heart. The thief would not be reminded of his stealing, nor the covetous man of his idolatry, nor the profane man of his cursing, nor the unconverted moral man of his wickedness in heart.

Oh, our churches do not win souls partly because they do not reach a crowd who need the Gospel. And again and a-gain, I have proved in major campaigns all over America that preaching on the scarlet sin, preaching on the death penalty for murder, preaching on the double curse of booze, and on other specific sins, has brought great crowds of lost people and has been used to win many to Christ. Some may come to scoff and remain to pray; some may be angry, but some will be blessed. A crowd will gather for a fight. And the preacher who makes an open, sharp, logical and scrip-tural attack on sin, specific sins of people who are involved, will find that many such people can be gotten to hear such preaching.

Again, preaching against sin leads people to conviction of sin. Often in a blessed revival campaign I have proved, as have the best evangelists in America, that a whole commu-nity may become conscious of sin, burdened about sin, and a moral revolution may take place because a preacher preached strongly against sin, showed its ruin, called people's attention to examples of what sin does for a man, for his family, for a community--that the whole climate was made favorable to the Gospel and a moral revolution took place in the city.

In an Oklahoma town, the newspaper publicly commented on the strange fact that during my three weeks' campaign not a single person had spent a night in jail.

In Decatur, Texas, a druggist attended the services in a ten weeks' campaign and publicly told how when his father had died, he had taken over the drug store and found that not a Bible was offered for sale in the entire county. He bought six hundred dollars' worth of Bibles and put them in stock. They lay on the shelves for years unbought, unread. During my campaign they sold out, and twice he restocked during the ten weeks' campaign, so great was the concern about the Bible and the Christian religion throughout the city.

In Greenville, South Carolina, in our city-wide campaign in Textile Hall, God mercifully brought conviction on a wide area. The newspaper columnist reported that as he talked to the manager of the Woolworth store, a boy came in and tearfully inquired for the manager. He must pay 45¢ for nine packs of chewing gum he had stolen. The columnist told that story to a floorwalker in Belk's Department Store and learned that here, too, people had come confessing their shoplifting, returning stolen goods or paying for them.

Preaching never brings a moral revolution unless there is an outright attack on sin, preached in the power of the Holy Spirit and with the authority of the Bible. No wonder that in such cases conviction mounts, individuals become burdened about their sins. Some cannot sleep and some come to the meetings purposely to get saved.

In one of our campaigns in Moncton, New Brunswick, such deep settled conviction was felt over the area covered by daily radio broadcasts and spread by those who attended the meetings nightly in the high school auditorium that people drove in from forty miles away expressly to be saved, and

352 found Christ in fifteen days. I am saying that churches do not win souls because there is no plain, strong, spirited, scriptural preaching against sin to bring people to conviction of sin and cause them to repent.

Again, let me say that the right kind of preaching may cause the preacher misunderstanding and criticism. He will have pressure by the officials of the church, by prominent members; pressure in his own family. He may find that the right kind of preaching against sin will bring a crucifixion in his own heart. It is still true that preachers ought to preach according to the Bible standard, whatever the cost. Churches do not win souls because preachers so often trim the corners. We do not harvest a crop because we do not kill the weeds. We do not make a good seedbed for the gospel seed because we plow around the stumps instead of digging them out.

VIII. Churches Often Do Not Win Souls Because the Preaching Is Not Spirit-Filled

Lack of the power of God surely must be the most important single cause of failure in the ministry. I know many well-trained preachers with college and seminary degrees who have few people saved. I know of men with charming personality who are good administrators, sensible leaders, yet they have few people saved. Why? Because they do not have the outpouring of the Spirit of God on their ministry.

We should remember that it was prophesied of Jesus in Isaiah 61:1 and fulfilled, "The Spirit of the Lord is upon me, because he hath anointed me to preach..." (Luke 4:18). The ministry of Jesus was powerful, not because He was the Son of God, though He was and is, but because He, as a Spirit-filled Man, showed us an example of how to work. His ministry was in the power of the Holy Spirit.

So the disciples were commanded, "Tarry ye in the city of Jerusalem, until ye be endued with power from on high" (Luke 24:49). Theologians would rather think about Pente-

cost as the origin of the church or as a dispensational matter. Some would prefer to think of the tongues or foreign
languages. Still others would prefer to make the Pentecostal experience "sanctification." But what they waited for
was to be endued with power from on high. And Jesus promised it again in Acts 1:8, "But ye shall receive power, after
that the Holy Ghost is come upon you: and ye shall be witnesses unto me both in Jerusalem, and in all Judaea, and in
Samaria, and unto the uttermost part of the earth." That
promise goes beyond Pentecost, and far beyond Jerusalem,
to the end of the nations and the end of the world. Lest anybody should think that the pouring out of the Holy Spirit at
Pentecost was an unrepeatable event, he should remember
that Acts 2:4, speaking of Pentecost, says, "And they were
all filled with the Holy Ghost," and Acts 4:31 tells about the
same people at a later time and again says, "And when they
had prayed, the place was shaken where they were assembled together; and they were all filled with the Holy Ghost."

When Paul was converted, Ananias came to him and prayed
for him that he might "be filled with the Holy Ghost" (Acts
9:17). Barnabas was a good soul winner because "he was a
good man, and full of the Holy Ghost and of faith: and much
people was added unto the Lord" (Acts 11:24). John the Baptist was a mighty soul winner because of this same enduement of power. "He shall be filled with the Holy Ghost, even
from his mother's womb. And many of the children of Israel shall he turn to the Lord their God" (Luke 1:15, 16).

Preachers do not win souls because they are not endued
with the mighty power of God. They are afraid of fanaticism, afraid of criticism. They retreat from extremists.
Preachers would rather spend time in study than in prayer.
They seek human means to win souls and carry on the
church work instead of the supernatural anointing which is
essential. Oh, the preacher who does not have upon him
the mighty power of the Holy Spirit will be fruitless until he
does! And if he has small power, he will have small re-

sults. The mighty soul-winning results among Bible Christians were by Spirit-filled men; so it must be today. Now let me say in closing the chapter that we cannot fix our churches until we fix our preachers. The preaching in our churches is often not the kind that takes a bold, strong leadership for God in the church. The preaching pleases men but does not please God. The preaching does not set a standard for soul winning, does not clean out the worldliness and train the workers for soul winning. The preaching does not make a strong issue of the fundamentals of the faith. It does not condemn sin, does not get the crowd of lost people that could be reached, does not bring conviction, does not get the hardened sinner saved. Worst of all, our preaching is largely powerless because it is not Spirit-filled preaching.

Let each pastor who reads this honestly search his heart. Are you largely responsible for the powerlessness and fruitlessness in your church?

6. Formalism Does Not Fit a Soul-Winning Church

On the front-page heading of every issue of THE SWORD OF THE LORD are these words: "An Independent Christian Weekly, Standing for the Verbal Inspiration of the Bible, the Deity of Christ, His Blood Atonement, Salvation by Faith, New Testament Soul Winning and the Premillennial Return of Christ. Opposes Modernism, Worldliness and Formalism."

THE SWORD OF THE LORD is an evangelistic paper. Through this weekly magazine which publishes at least one sermon to the unsaved each week, along with other sermons, and through other books and pamphlets which the Sword promotes, over twelve thousand letters have come from people who wrote saying that they here and now take Christ as Saviour. Now why does this magazine, devoted to soul winning and greatly used of God in winning souls and in promoting soul winning, commit itself, "Opposes Modernism, Worldliness and Formalism"? Because in the experience and conviction of the best soul winners everywhere, modernism, worldliness and formalism are akin and all hinder soul winning.

When churches lose their evangelistic fervor, then forms and ceremonies take the place of the zeal and power which are now lacking. In Rome, when New Testament simplicity and power and evangelism changed into that unscriptural monster, the Roman Church, the forms became more elaborate, rich and awesome as the orthodoxy and New Testament doctrine and power disappeared! Instead of simple meetings in homes or lofts or by the seaside or in the streets, now great and elaborate buildings appeared. Instead of simple preachers teaching and preaching the Gospel, as New Testament preachers did, there appeared elaborately robed priests, rich jewels, candles, incense, along with the doctrine of salvation by works and by the church and by ceremonies and through a priesthood. When they turned from baptism as the public confession of faith on the part of a penitent sinner, buried in the likeness of Christ's burial and raised to live in newness of life following Christ's pattern, then baptism became a saving ordinance, and was practiced even on unconscious babies and unregenerate sinners. Instead of being a simple memorial supper reminding Christians of the death of Christ for their sins, the Lord's Supper became to them an elaborate sacrament of the church, a new sacrifice of Christ, or a "means of grace," even as it is regarded among many Protestant groups.

As every major group of Christians or professing Christians have gone away from New Testament simplicity, orthodoxy and soul winning, they have gone into more elaborate ritual and formalism. Formalism is itself the opposite of Bible Christianity and has always marked the departure from soul winning.

So Christians and the pastor and church may make the decision: They may have the formalism and please men, or they can have New Testament Christianity and simplicity and win souls and please God. But the more of formalism, the less of soul winning. Formalism hinders soul winning.

I. How Prevalent Is Formality in the Churches That Win Few or No Souls!

It is bad for the liturgical churches, Catholics, Episcopalians, Lutherans, and others who have priests, who claim baptismal regeneration for babies and who have memorized prayers and who openly teach either that there is saving merit or at least a "means of grace" in the ceremony--it is bad for them to have their forms and ceremonies, and surely any pastor and people who want to win souls can see that this formalism in its extremity, as practiced by Catholics and the liturgical Protestant churches, does not tend toward soul winning.

But now formalism has spread so widely that even the churches that claim to be orthodox and evangelical and fundamental often follow the forms that fit Catholics but do not fit Protestants, and fit modernists but do not fit fundamental, Bible-believing people and churches. Now churches regularly announce a "Morning Worship Service" and "Evening Worship." Pastors say, "We will now worship God with our tithes and offerings." Even in orthodox circles, people are counseled to go to church "to worship," whether the preaching brings any blessing or not! "Worship," as it is now used, does not imply beseeching prayer, asking God for things and getting them, but meditation, perhaps adoration and pious feeling, without any practical or objective help or gain. The singing need not have any Gospel in it; the preaching need not aim at conversion of sinners nor changing of Christians. It may be simply "Gather around the Word" for some self-righteous enjoyment at best; or at worst to tolerate as brief a sermon as possible and gain a Pharisee's self-righteous self-esteem!

The Sunday morning service particularly is a time for people to wear their finest clothes and sit with funeral solemnity and follow a printed schedule from which they dare not deviate. Only at certain times in the service may people be seated. There is a set time to stand and a set time to sit. The preacher prays a formal prayer, often one that is written out, and the choir chants a response or perhaps a four-fold or seven-fold amen!

If our churches are to win many souls the preachers must renounce this false concept of a "worship service" and return to the informality of the New Testament churches, the constant soul-winning emphasis. There are times for the pastor (as for other individual Christians), to prostrate himself before God on his face in "worship" privately. But there were no "worship services" in the New Testament in the formal sense.

The so-called "morning worship service" must be an abomination to God. Nothing like it was practiced in New Testament times. There is not a verse of Scripture to encourage it. It is sensual and carnal, not spiritual. The formality of the usual Sunday morning service fits with modernism but not with fundamentalism. It is suitable for Catholics but not for Protestants. Nobody expects a sinner to get converted in a formal so-called "worship service" and they are not disappointed.

The Pharisee Jesus described in Luke, chapter 18, would have felt very much at home in a morning worship service. Robed choir, beautiful organ, anthems--sometimes by paid singers, very often by worldly and ungodly singers, but aesthetically pleasing--would have suited him very well. He would have liked the hush, the so-called "reverence." He would have enjoyed the organ playing during prayer, because his kind of prayer would not get anything from God anyway, and would only please the hearers. The rising and sitting, the bowing and scraping, the set forms of the services, with no sinners called to repentance, with no Christians rebuked for worldliness, with no pointed application of Scripture, would have pleased the Pharisee very much. But the publican would not have come to such a service. In the first place, nobody would want him. In the second place, he would not feel at home. And in the third place, he would know that he could not get any help there. Formality does not save souls.

The music in the Sunday morning "formal worship service" must usually include anthems and always, of course, the "Gloria Patri" (the Latin name itself shows that it is patterned after Rome) or the Doxology and probably "Holy, Holy, Holy." Songs must usually be about God ("Jesus, you can get into the Sunday evening services"). They must not be evangelistic, for the "Gospel song" certainly does not fit "morning worship service." There may be a choir director in the evening service when only a handful is present (until the formal church finally drops the Sunday evening service). But no waving of the arm nor leading people in a happy song Sunday morning! That would not fit the funeral parlor atmosphere. And in many churches, the piano may not be used on Sunday morning. That is entirely too informal and might encourage too much rhythm and happiness in the singing. No, it must be the organ because the great cathedrals and the Roman and Episcopal and Lutheran churches have organs and organists (usually a professional paid organist). The piano is all right for the young people's meeting and for some of the other services, but for the "formal worship service" all tradition is for the organ. And announcements and promotion of services to get lost people out and get people saved? No, no--not Sunday morning!

As a guest of The Evangelical Foreign Mission Association, I went to Japan to speak in their annual Bible conference at Karuizawa, a mountain resort where missionaries gather in the summer. To six hundred missionaries I preached on soul winning in the power of the Holy Spirit for a week.

A week preceding I had spent with the national Japanese pastors. At one time some eight hundred of these pastors had been taking THE SWORD OF THE LORD. We have had millions of copies of some eight or nine of my books and pamphlets translated in Japanese, so the Japanese pastors love me, and a committee of pastors started a movement to celebrate three years later, in 1959, the one hundredth anniversary of the coming of missionaries to Japan. They approached me and Dr. Fred Jarvis. They wanted me to conduct city-wide campaigns in principal cities. They wanted me to publish another million copies of my booklet, "What Must I Do to Be Saved?" in Japanese. They offered to enlist a great team of soul-winning preachers who would go anywhere for revival campaigns if someone would pay traveling and living expenses. They appealed to noble missionary Dr. Fred Jarvis and to me, to see if we would help them get this great nationwide celebration under way, would help them raise money, would help them organize, help get literature ready.

Dr. Jarvis and I agreed and counseled with other missionaries, and it was determined that on Monday night following this great annual Bible conference of six hundred evangelical missionaries, they would have a banquet. All the missionaries were invited. Dr. Jarvis and I would take care of the expenses. They would join in with national pastors for a great nationwide emphasis on revival and soul winning during the one hundredth anniversary of missions in Japan.

All to whom we talked were enthusiastic about it. But Dr. Jarvis and I talked to the chairman of the meeting. Could we make announcements on Sunday morning about that big banquet on Monday night to which all missionaries were invited, and a matter in which all of them were favorably inclined? The chairman was nonplussed. Well, he would have to see the program committee. The program committee was doubtful.

Dr. Jarvis and I insisted that on this matter they were all agreed that it was right and that it ought to be promoted. But the chairman turned in deepest distress to me and said, "But Dr. Rice! It is Sunday morning!" Because of the tradition of the formal Sunday morning service, this missionary, who had pledged his life to mission work and representing six hundred other missionaries who had pledged themselves as fundamental, Bible-believing missionaries, felt it would be a disgrace to have a public announcement on Sunday morning here in the meeting of the missionaries themselves!

I preached in a large Denver church to an audience of some nine hundred, I suppose. Those of us on the platform and in the choir could see what took place in the back. Before the ushers came forward for the offering, they stood

like soldiers, perfectly poised, left foot ready to step, while
the chairman of the deacons stood back there with arm
raised to Heaven. When he brought it swiftly down, then
they marched toward the front in perfect unison. I thought
of the "Rangerettes"--that great group of girls from Kilgore
College in Texas who, with cowboy hats and shorts, march
like that at football games. Don't misunderstand me. I love
order. I was in the army. I could take a company of soldiers, drill them and march them across the parade ground
today, with the military bands playing Sousa's "Stars and
Stripes Forever." I delight in rhythmic motion; neverthe-
less, that is not New Testament Christianity. It has nothing
good to do with soul winning, but only distracts the mind and
sets religion in a certain formal pattern where the Gospel
does not easily reach sinners and where sinners are not
much impressed with it.

I have seen a little struggling congregation in a rented
store building, with perhaps only forty people present, try
to practice the same forms and ceremonies on Sunday
morning because that was supposed to be the thing to do!

The prevalence of formalism in worship is the enemy of
soul winning, and no formal church wins very many souls.

And the church that tries to have a formal worship service Sunday morning will have cultivated an attitude among
the people so that the other services will be tainted with the
same ideas and the similar powerlessness will prevail.

I am somewhat familiar with the best soul-winning churches and pastors in America. Seven men on the Co-operating
Board of Sword of the Lord Foundation, of which I am president, are pastors of great churches and baptize a total of
about 5,400 converts each year. These are not formal
churches, but great informal, Bible-believing, soul-winning churches.

I know that there are books written with chapters on how
to conduct a formal worship service. But they are not books
on soul winning, and the men who write them are not prom-

inent as soul winners. There are perhaps ten churches in America that baptize over three hundred converts a year. There are, it is said, only some twenty churches that baptize two hundred converts a year. And none of them have distinctly formal services even on Sunday morning. They have announcements; they have gospel singing; they have sermons to the unsaved and public invitation to accept Christ.

II. The Formal Worship Service Wholly Unknown in the New Testament

Worship in the Bible means usually to kneel down or to prostrate one's self. So Satan tempted Christ to "fall down and worship me" (Matt. 4:9; Luke 4:7). In I Corinthians 14:25 we are told that if all God's people witness in the power of the Spirit (prophesy), a lost sinner will be convicted and "falling down on his face he will worship God."

The word worship is used about heathen worship: "Them that worship the host of heaven" (Zeph. 1:5). The Samaritan woman said, "Our fathers worshipped in this mountain" (John 4:20). In Acts 17:23 at Athens Paul said, speaking of the altar "TO THE UNKNOWN GOD," "Whom therefore ye ignorantly worship, him declare I unto you." In Jeremiah 44:19, the idolatrous women, speaking of the queen of Heaven, said, "Did we make her cakes to worship her...without our men?"

But the word worship is never used about a service where there was preaching, where Christians sang praises together, studied the Word of God together or won souls together. It is not mentioned in connection with New Testament church meetings or services, not a single time! So worship in the Bible usually means physical prostration, simply bowing down or falling down on the face before someone. In other cases, it represents heathen worship, forms and ceremonies. But the term is never used for singing, preaching, soul winning, Bible study and Bible teaching, and Christian fellowship such as the New Testament churches had.

The formal worship service came not from the Bible but from Catholicism. It is carnal, not spiritual. It is from human wisdom, not by divine revelation. It is man-pleasing, not God-obeying. Catholics got the germ of some of their ceremonies from the Old Testament. Not realizing that the Old Testament priesthood was simply an object lesson pointing toward Christ, they take the priesthood instead of Christ. They try to receive Christ in the mouth through the wafer instead of in the heart by simple faith. And instead of preachers, they have priests to lord it over God's people, to administer God's salvation or withhold it. They put merit in the sign of the cross, in prayers to Mary, in climbing holy stairs or burning expensive candles or in doing without meat on Fridays and dieting during Lent. But there is as much paganism adopted into Romanism as there is Old Testament symbolism, and all of it together is contrary to the New Testament and hateful to God, and it shuts out New Testament soul winning. I do not say that no one is ever saved in a Catholic, Episcopal, or Lutheran church, or in some other formal service. I say that soul winning is so greatly hindered that it is almost nonexistent, and that salvation is rare with such a background.

Even the ceremonies of the Old Testament became hateful to God when the people did not understand the meaning of them and there was no heart devotion and faith along with the observance. And so, in Isaiah 1:1-15, God says to Israel:

"The vision of Isaiah the son of Amoz, which he saw concerning Judah and Jerusalem in the days of Uzziah, Jotham, Ahaz, and Hezekiah, kings of Judah. Hear, O heavens, and give ear, O earth: for the Lord hath spoken, I have nourished and brought up children, and they have rebelled against me. The ox knoweth his owner, and the ass his master's crib: but Israel doth not know, my people doth not consider. Ah sinful nation, a people laden with iniquity, a seed of evildoers, children that are corrupters: they have forsaken the Lord, they have provoked the Holy One of Israel unto anger, they are gone away backward. Why should ye be stricken any more? ye will revolt more and more: the whole head is sick, and the whole heart faint. From the sole of the foot even unto the head there is no soundness in it; but wounds, and bruises, and putrifying sores: they have not been closed, neither bound up, neither mollified with ointment. Your country is desolate, your cities are burned with fire: your land, strangers devour it in your presence, and it is desolate, as overthrown by strangers. And the daughter of Zion is left as a cottage in a vineyard, as a lodge in a garden of cucumbers, as a besieged city. Except the Lord of hosts had left unto us a very small remnant, we should have been as Sodom, and we should have been like unto Gomorrah. Hear the word of the Lord, ye rulers of Sodom; give ear unto the law of our God, ye people of Gomorrah. To what purpose is the multitude of your sacrifices unto me? saith the Lord: I am full of the burnt-offerings of rams, and the fat of fed beasts; and I delight not in the blood of bullocks, or of lambs, or of he goats. When ye come to appear before me, who hath required this at your hand, to tread my courts? Bring no more vain oblations; incense is an abomination unto me; the new moons and sabbaths, the calling of assemblies, I cannot away with; it is iniquity, even the solemn meeting. Your new moons and your appointed feasts my soul hateth: they are a trouble unto me; I am weary to bear them. And when ye spread forth your hands, I will hide mine eyes from you: yea, when ye make many prayers, I will not hear: your hands are full of blood."

The Lord says, "Bring no more vain oblations; incense is an abomination unto me." He says, "Your new moons and your appointed feasts my soul hateth: they are a trouble unto me; I am weary to bear them."

Even in the Old Testament time it was not the ceremonies themselves that pleased God, but only the heart attitude, if they saw and loved the truth pictured. He said to them in the three following verses:

"Wash you, make you clean; put away the evil of your doings from before mine eyes; cease to do evil; Learn to do well; seek judgment, relieve the oppressed, judge the fatherless, plead for the widow. Come now, and let us reason together, saith the Lord: though your sins be as scarlet, they shall be as white as snow; though they be red like crimson, they shall be as wool."--Isa. 1:16-18.

We may be sure today that baptism is as abominable to God when it is not the response of a born-again, believing heart, as the bringing of incense was by an unconverted and ungodly Jew in the Old Testament. We may be sure that the people who take communion because they have learned the catechism or because it is thought to be "a means of grace," and take it with an unconverted heart, or take it with a worldly life, eat and drink to their own condemnation, as I Corinthians 11:29 says. So those who eat that bread and drink that cup should examine themselves first, we are told (vs. 28).

What does God want with songs of praise when there is no lilt in the heart? God must hate the beautiful Episcopal "prayer of general confession" (and it is beautiful and orthodox), when it is chanted by lips that take God's name in vain, and as a ceremony when there is no heart confession or heart repentance, and done by unconverted people!

How sharply the Saviour criticized the Pharisees and Sadducees, the chief priests and rulers of the Jews, quoting Isaiah 29:13, "Well hath Esaias prophesied of you hypocrites, as it is written, This people honoureth me with their lips, but their heart is far from me" (Mark 7:6).

But the ceremonies of the Old Testament are now done away. When Jesus died on the cross, the veil of the Temple was torn from top to bottom. God was saying that now the types have been fulfilled and Jesus, grieving over Jerusalem, said, "Your house is left unto you desolate" (Matt. 23:38). The Shekinah Glory no more lives within the Temple at Jerusalem. The Temple itself was to be destroyed, its usefulness over, when Titus destroyed Jerusalem in A. D. 70. And the sacrifices, the lambs, the turtledoves, pigeons, bullocks, scapegoats? All done! All over! Now by one offering the Lord "hath perfected for ever them that are sanctified" (Heb. 10:14). Now the law is written in the heart and "there is no more offering for sin" (vs. 18). Even when the Old Testament ceremonies were in order as object lessons and types, they were an abomination when people came with unbelieving, cold hearts; now they are utterly done away and to return to the law is to fall from grace, that is, fall from the Bible doctrine of grace (Gal. 5:4).

III. Jesus Said It Is Hypocrisy in Seeking to Please or Impress Men When We Serve God

Formalism in religion is intended to affect men, not to affect God. But that is deceitful and Jesus again and again calls doing things to be seen or heard of men as hypocrisy. So it is about giving alms. He said:

> "Take heed that ye do not your alms before men, to be seen of them: otherwise ye have no reward of your Father which is in heaven. Therefore when thou doest thine alms, do not sound a trumpet before thee, as the hypocrites do in the synagogues and in the streets, that they may have glory of men. Verily I say unto you, They have their reward. But when thou doest alms, let not thy left hand know what thy right hand doeth: That thine alms may be in secret: and thy Father which seeth in secret himself shall reward thee openly."--Matt. 6:1-4.

What is the sin here? It is that men give "that they may

have glory of men." It is "before men, to be seen of them." Jesus said about this " . . . as the hypocrites do." The beauty about giving that is done in secret is that it is done to please God and is certain to have His reward. The great temptation about giving in public is that it is likely to be done to be seen of men, to have the glory of men, and thus it has no divine reward. Such giving pretends to be to please God, when actually it is to impress and please men.

Jesus said this similar thing about praying in Matthew 6:5-8:

> "And when thou prayest, thou shalt not be as the hypo-crites are: for they love to pray standing in the syna-gogues and in the corners of the streets, that they may be seen of men. Verily I say unto you, They have their reward. But thou, when thou prayest, enter into thy closet, and when thou hast shut thy door, pray to the Fa-ther which is in secret; and thy Father which seeth in secret shall reward thee openly. But when ye pray, use not vain repetitions, as the heathen do; for they think that they shall be heard for their much speaking. Be not ye therefore like unto them: for your Father knoweth what things ye have need of, before ye ask him."

Again, what is the complaint Jesus has with the way hypo-crites pray? "That they may be seen of men."

In a revival campaign a pastor told me, "Sister _____ is able in prayer. You may call on her sometime if you wish." I never called on her. The Lord deliver me from those "who are able in prayer." Their eloquent language pleases men, but that makes it the less likely to please God. So most of our praying should be secret praying. And when we have public prayer, one should be very careful to lead the people in actual, simple petition to God.

In this connection the Lord gave warning, "Use not vain repetitions, as the heathen do" (Matt. 6:7). Yes, and as Catholics and Episcopalians and others who have set prayers. In a revival campaign when I preached in a morning service on prayer, a lady present was secretary of a pastor of another church. This service was in October; she told me that her pastor had dictated to her his morning prayers through the next March--six months ahead of time! All he had to do was to pick one of these typed prayers and when the people bowed their heads, he could read it. That was "vain repetition." That was like the heathen who think "they shall be heard for their much speaking." Is God more likely to hear a prayer written out in beautiful ear-pleasing language? No. That is done for the ears of men, not necessarily for God.

Years ago, in a mass meeting in Tremont Temple in Boston, the daily paper reported, "The Reverend Dr. So and So pronounced the invocation. It was probably the most eloquent prayer ever addressed to a Boston audience." If that was so, then that man was a hypocrite. He was speaking to impress men when he pretended to please God. And that kind of formalism is an abomination which Jesus here plainly forbids.

On the matter of fasting, again Jesus said:

> "Moreover when ye fast, be not, as the hypocrites, of a sad countenance: for they disfigure their faces, that they may appear unto men to fast. Verily I say unto you, They have their reward. But thou, when thou fastest, anoint thine head, and wash thy face; That thou appear not unto men to fast, but unto thy Father which is in secret: and thy Father, which seeth in secret, shall reward thee openly."--Matt. 6:16-18.

Again Jesus said on this matter, "Be not, as the hypocrites." It is hypocrisy when men fast that they may "appear unto men to fast." Such people already have their reward. I suspect that not many of my readers ever fast, but at least the Lord is saying here, as He said repeatedly in the sixth chapter of Matthew, that any religious observance done to be seen of men, to be heard of men, to have glory of men, to impress men, is hypocrisy, is as the heathen do, and does not please God. It is plainly forbidden.

Also, any routine and rote matter of religious "worship" is forbidden, is vain repetitions, that is, repeating words that do not come from the heart, or repeating songs that do not come from the heart, or observing the Lord's Supper or baptism where the heart is not involved. All such vain repetition, such formalism, Jesus Christ has forbidden.

IV. The Formal Emphasis on Church Buildings and Sacred Things Hinders Soul Winning

Unfortunately, our conception of a beautiful church building is taken from the great cathedrals in Europe with their Gothic arches, their high domes and steeples, their flying buttresses, their stained glass windows. The largest church building in the world and the grandest, I suppose, is St. Peter's at Rome, over 600 feet long, with a dome 404 feet high. It is filled with rich statuary, beautiful religious paintings, beautiful columns with inlaid work and gold, with many altars. Although the ecumenical council of bishops and cardinals were meeting there and so much of it was temporarily seated for them when we were there in the spring, it is regularly not seated, it is not a place for preaching or soul winning. So it is largely with the famous St. Paul's and Westminster Abbey in London. People have tried to make the church buildings into temples with the riches and imagery like the Old Testament Temple. It is an emphasis on buildings and places and things, which is wholly foreign to New Testament Christianity and does not fit in with the Great Commission and the appointed work of New Testament Christians and churches.

The Crusades wasted the richest blood of Europe trying to take back the land of Palestine as if the land itself were holy. Legend and history loves to deal with the search for the Holy Grail, that is, for the cup which tradition says

Jesus used in founding the Lord's Supper. Queen Helena, the mother of Emperor Constantine, went to Palestine and selected places she thought were authentic for the birth of Christ, for the crucifixion and burial, and for the home of Joseph and Mary in Nazareth, and there she had churches erected. There is no evidence but long, cultivated Catholic tradition that Jesus was born in that cave at Bethlehem. But Helena thought, as millions of others have thought, that the place would be more honored if a great church were built on the spot--so the Church of the Holy Sepulchre in Jerusalem. I think it is not at the correct place, but if it were, it would be more useful if it were not prostituted with a great building to please the eye of worldly men and draw them away from the Bible account of the crucifixion and salvation by the blood of Christ.

Queen Helena, tradition says, brought twenty-eight marble stairs that she thought were taken from Pilate's judgment hall (destroyed by Titus in A. D. 70), to Rome. They are now installed in the Church of St. John the Lateran in Rome. And people climb these stairs on their knees; with tears they kiss each step, thinking thus to gain favor with God.

And over much of Europe there are kept so-called "sacred relics"--reputed nails from the true cross, a cloth with which, tradition says, Jesus wiped His face and left the bloody print of His face on the cloth, "pieces of the true cross," a bit of hair from the head of the Virgin Mary or bones from this saint or that. Rome makes much of the supposed bones of Peter which they hope they have found in Rome. Naturally, there is no evidence in the Bible or in history that Peter ever was in Rome, but much evidence that he was not there. Paul did not know it and it is never mentioned in the letter to Rome nor in letters from Rome, nor did Paul mention it, nor others. Alas the churches too much have absorbed this human and carnal way of making much of religious places, buildings and things.

V. No Church Building Takes Place of Old Testament Temple

It is true that God had His people build a rich Temple in the time of King Solomon and millions of treasures were used there. It is true also that in that Temple, as it was in the wilderness Tabernacle before, there was a holy of holies and a mercy seat covering the ark or chest of God. In that chest was originally the two tables of stone on which God wrote the Ten Commandments, Aaron's rod that budded and bore almonds, and a sample pot of the manna in the wilderness, miraculously preserved through the centuries. More important still, the living presence of God, the Shekinah Glory, dwelt in that most holy place. There was a living flame above the mercy seat. We think it was the same as that pillar of fire in the wilderness over the Tabernacle in the night and the pillar of cloud by day, which went before and led the way for Israel. When it moved, they followed; when it stopped, they camped.

Ah, but thank God that Temple is gone and we have far better! The sacrifices there had no meaning after Jesus was crucified. No wonder "the veil of the temple was rent in twain from the top to the bottom" (Matt. 27:51); and Jesus said, "O Jerusalem...your house is left unto you desolate" (Matt. 23:37, 38).

In John 4, the woman in Samaria said, "Our fathers worshipped in this mountain; and ye say, that in Jerusalem is the place where men ought to worship." But Jesus answered her, "Woman, believe me, the hour cometh, when ye shall neither in this mountain, nor yet at Jerusalem, worship the Father....But the hour cometh and now is, when the true worshippers shall worship the Father in spirit and in truth: for the Father seeketh such to worship him" (John 4:21, 23). From His words, the Lord Jesus makes clear that God will not attach Himself to a place. Once Daniel in far-off Babylon would open his window toward Jerusalem and pray toward that Temple, that place, but no more. God now has something far better for Christians.

Now the temple of God, the only temple God has on earth, is the body of a Christian. First Corinthians 6:19, 20 says, "What? know ye not that your body is the temple of the Holy Ghost which is in you, which ye have of God, and ye are not your own? For ye are bought with a price: therefore glorify God in your body, and in your spirit, which are God's."

And again I Corinthians 3:16, 17 warns us: "Know ye not that ye are the temple of God, and that the Spirit of God dwelleth in you? If any man defile the temple of God, him shall God destroy; for the temple of God is holy, which temple ye are."

O Christian, your body is the temple of God, the only temple He has on earth!

On the proscenium arch of a church auditorium are sometimes found these words of Scripture: "The Lord is in his holy temple: let all the earth keep silence before him" (Hab. 2:20). But that command about the Temple at Jerusalem does not fit a church building. We call church buildings "the house of God," but actually God does not live there. The church building is no more the house of God than the home of a Christian is. It is true that a church building may be built with the sacrificial and loving gifts of God's people to God, and the building may be dedicated to His service. However, my own home ought to be as definitely given to God and used for His glory as a church building. People write me, as an editor and Bible teacher, to answer the question, "What do you think of churches serving meals in the house of God?" I answer that anything that can be done in a church house to glorify the Lord is all right, on exactly the same standards that one would use in serving God in his own home. I quote I Corinthians 10:31: "Whether therefore ye eat, or drink, or whatsoever ye do, do all to the glory of God." I think it is a mistake for church groups to be too much occupied with social affairs, if it subtracts from soul winning. But if a Mother-and-Daughter banquet can bring unsaved people to hear the Gospel in a church building, well

and good! If God's people can arrange to leave their work
and hasten to the church house for a simple meal while they
prepare to go on house-to-house visitation, thus making it
possible for some to come who otherwise could not, well
and good.

Again let me stress it: the church building is not a temple. It is not the home of God. God does not live there. The
temple of God on earth is the body of a Christian and that is
the only temple that God has on earth.

Pastors have grown a custom, along with the growth of
formalism, of calling the church auditorium "the sanctuary."
Thus men distinguish between the church auditorium and
Sunday school rooms and offices in a church house, as if it
were specially sacred because God is in the auditorium and
meets His people there. In many churches "the altar" is
counted sacred, and it may be expensively carved or inlaid
or adorned with a gold cross or priceless cloth. Actually
the church building properly has no altar. It has a pulpit
for preaching. It may have a convenient place for sinners
to kneel and be shown the Word of God and be taught to pray
the penitent's prayer, but, thank God, the altar of the Christians is on that little hill shaped like a skull, Calvary, and
the great offering of the precious blood has already been
made, and "there is no more offering for sin" (Heb. 10:18).
People are falsely taught that there is a special virtue in
bringing their gifts and money to that altar in the church
building. It is not so. God is often more pleased if the
alms are given in secret to the brother who needs it. The
ministry of the church ought to be supported by God's people, but there is no more virtue in having it presented before a "worship center" or a church "altar" than in turning
it in in an envelope in a Sunday school class, or handing it
to the minister, or any other sensible and business-like way
to attend to God's business.

People are taught in these days of formalism and religion
that one of the greatest virtues of a Christian is to have

"reverence for the house of God." Sometimes on a church bulletin, or on a sign in the foyer, are these words, "If you must whisper, whisper a prayer." And people are exhorted to be silent and reverent while the organ plays. Actually God would much more be honored and the purpose of the churches and the command of Christ much more honored by greeting visitors gladly and happily, seeing that they were comfortably seated and that they felt welcome, than the funeral silence which formalism dictates.

The formal emphasis on the church building, church furniture, Gothic arches, stained glass windows, robed choir, is a false emphasis, contrary to the spiritual facts and a deadly influence on soul winning.

As far as the Scripture records show, there was not a single church building in the entire New Testament time. In Jerusalem the people met in the plaza, or on Solomon's porch, near the Temple. They met in people's homes. When Peter and John healed a lame man at the Beautiful gate of the Temple in Acts 3, Peter preached there in the street, as he did again and again. Preachers preached in the homes of the people. In Troas Paul preached in a loft. In their journeys Paul and Barnabas preached in the synagogues and then, when driven from the synagogues, preached in people's homes, in public market places. Paul at Athens preached at Mars' Hill among the idols. He preached by the campfire among the barbarians on the Island of Melita (Malta) after he was shipwrecked. He preached to the Jewish leaders assembled at his prison house in Rome.

The simple truth is that down through history, in great periods of soul winning, the multitudes have been saved outside of church buildings more often than in them.

Think of the great revivals by Wesley and by Whitefield with the "field preaching," when they sometimes preached to ten thousand or twenty thousand people! In his autobiography Benjamin Franklin tells how when Whitefield came to America and preached in the streets of Philadelphia to multitudes, he figured that the way Whitefield's voice carried in the open air, he could be heard by thirty thousand people standing in the streets!

Think of the great revivals of D. L. Moody in giant tabernacles, in great auditoriums, in the circus tent at the Chicago World's Fair. Remember the Billy Sunday campaigns in great board tabernacles all over America.

And I am glad for the tens of thousands who claimed Christ in my own poor ministry. I am sure that God was as much pleased with those saved in Kleinhans Music Hall at Buffalo, the Public Music Hall in Cleveland, the City Auditorium in Miami, in the Binghamton Theater in Binghamton, or in the giant Liberty Tobacco Warehouse in Winston-Salem, as He was pleased with people saved in any church building in the world!

It is strikingly true that the more people emphasize rich buildings and sacred places, the less fruitful evangelism there is. Some of us on the tour of Bible lands were shown through Westminster Abbey in London. It was during Lent, and so the bishop had decided there ought to be public services in the Abbey. So as the rector, with his robe and with his collar buttoned behind, intoned his sermon, two people, only two, sat where they could have heard him, but seemed not to care. Others of us were shown through the Abbey, walking and speaking somewhat quietly out of respect to the people. But I am certain that that ancient place, where the great of England are buried and where the Queen was crowned, does not see as many souls saved as any one of thousands of little unpretentious church buildings or with congregations meeting in a rented store building or in a revival tent. I doubt if any are ever saved there. One of the heartbreaks of going through Palestine is to see that there, walking where the Saviour walked and talked and preached and suffered and died and rose again--there, with monks and priests everywhere and churches over every so-called sacred spot, there is practically no Gospel preached and very few sinners ever hear that they can personally trust Christ and be saved at once. I preached in Jerusalem to a congregation of some thirty-two people, in an auditorium made from two rooms of a home and sadly heard that there were only two or three such places in Jerusalem itself where the Gospel was regularly preached and that to only a few!

Let me say it again: Formality fits Rome, not Protestantism; fits modernism, not fundamental Bible faith and service; fits cults teaching salvation by works or priesthood or ceremonies; it does not fit simple New Testament churches teaching salvation by grace through faith.

Formalism hinders soul winning.

7. How Formalism Hinders Soul Winning in the Churches

It is well to remember that in this poor fallen race of ours we must constantly guard against the downpull of our old carnal, fleshly natures. The flesh leads away from God, not toward God. So in every generation there is a decay of Bible Christianity and many fall far from the New Testament pattern.

And when people go wrong in essential doctrine, they go wrong in obedience to the Great Commission, and soul winning suffers. When people quit believing in the virgin birth and the bodily resurrection of Christ, they cease also winning souls. When people turn away from the moral standard of New Testament Christianity, they also turn away from the soul-winning power of God. And when people leave the spirit and practice of New Testament Christianity, they also diminish in soul winning.

So THE SWORD OF THE LORD every week announces on the front page that it "Opposes Modernism, Worldliness and Formalism." The churches whose principal expression is in great cathedrals, stained glass windows, Gothic arches, elaborate altars, in beautiful ritual, do not find soul winning a principal expression. To depart from the New Testament practice departs from New Testament soul winning.

Now may we suggest some ways that we think formalism in the church services hinders soul winning.

1. Sunday Morning "Worship Service" Prostitutes and Wastes the Best Opportunity of Winning Souls

The most fruitful time for winning souls in any church service is Sunday morning. In the great soul-winning churches in America, such as Temple Baptist Church in

Detroit, Highland Park Baptist in Chattanooga, First Baptist Church in Hammond, and a thousand more that I know, the greatest reaping of all the week is on Sunday morning. In the Hammond church about three-fourths of all public professions are on Sunday morning. A strong evangelistic church may have twenty public professions of faith Sunday morning, and but three or four on Sunday night, and possibly one to claim the Lord Jesus as Saviour on a Wednesday night or in a young people's meeting. But always the great reaping is on Sunday morning in the fruitful, soul-winning churches.

One reason for this is that everywhere more people go to church on Sunday morning than on Sunday night or on a week night. Many years ago D. L. Moody remarked that Sunday night was the best time for evangelism. That was true then. In old times, the unconverted, the general public, those who had no connection with the churches, would attend the strong and bold evangelistic preaching on Sunday night.

That is not generally true anywhere in America today. The churches that win many souls Sunday morning, may also have a good Sunday night service, but I do not know a single church which has a formal Sunday morning service and regularly a strong evangelistic, soul-saving service on Sunday night.

The general public feels that if they would go to church, they had better go Sunday morning. There are many things that clamor for their attention the rest of the day. In the evening they may watch a favorite TV program, or go to dinner at a popular restaurant, or spend the afternoon and evening at the beaches, or in the car. But the unchurched public, if it goes to a church house at all, will go Sunday morning.

Then, the Sunday school is the strongest single factor a church can have in getting the general public to attend a service. The Sunday school is the only organization in a church which can reach all the church constituency--its

members and friends. And such churches that have vig-
ourous, carefully supervised and spiritual Sunday schools,
can assemble the larger portion of the Sunday school attendance into the church auditorium to hear the preaching of
the Gospel in an evangelistic Sunday morning service. If
that service be formal, stiff, cold, instead of warmly informal and evangelistic, then lost people present are not likely
to be saved. And they are not likely to come again. And
church members who would like to win souls are not encouraged to bring lost people to such a service, hoping they
will find Christ. No, if the Sunday morning service is
wasted in a "formal worship service," the one great opportunity of the week for winning people to Christ or bringing
those who have trusted Christ through the visitation program out to make public profession of faith is lost. The
formal worship service is a deadly rival of the soul-winning
service.

I know that some preachers blandly say that they will have
a formal worship service Sunday morning but that the Sunday evening service will be evangelistic. But such preachers had as well face the honest fact which they have ignored
or excused: the church that isn't burdened for souls and
doesn't do all it can to win souls in the greatest opportunity
they will have on Sunday morning, will not suddenly be
changed into a red-hot evangelistic center on Sunday night!
The preacher who was more concerned about having a cultural and an aesthetic and man-pleasing service on Sunday
morning, will not suddenly be filled with the Holy Spirit for
Sunday night and burdened, weeping, pleading for souls! The
church that is not evangelistic Sunday morning will not be
evangelistic Sunday night.

No, the church which has a formal Sunday morning service has already announced to its members and to the world
that the form and ceremony are more important to it than
doing what Jesus commanded us to do in the Great Com-
mission--to try to get "every creature" saved.

II. Formalism in Services Leaves No Freedom for Soul Winning

Suppose a good Christian insists on one of his fellow workers at the shop coming with him to service. The Christian may go by for his friend and the family and gather them happily in his own car with his own wife and children. Or he may plan to meet them on the church steps at a certain time. Happily he takes this stranger in, sees that he meets other friendly, good men, or he sees that each one finds his place in the Sunday school, and then later finds them a good seat and sits with the strangers in the church auditorium. He introduces the man to the man in front of him, and to the one behind him.

The stranger feels welcomed and glad he came. These people are nice to him! They would be good friends! And when they sing, they sing some simple gospel song. Probably it is one he heard his mother sing, or one they sang in Sunday school when he was a boy. The pastor may have visitors stand and have someone hand them a card. The visitor will put his name and address on the card and somebody from the men's Bible class or the pastor will go by to see him during the following week. Or a teacher of junior boys will come by to see his son.

The sermon is earnest, warm, informal, but plain. Then there is a public invitation to take Christ as Saviour. The matter is made very plain. He is urged to turn in his heart now, from his sins, to trust the Lord Jesus and to come forward in open profession of faith. He is told plainly that someone will sit or kneel with him, will show him verses in the Bible, will pray with him and make sure that he fully understands and has assurance that his sins are forgiven. His friend beside him speaks in his ear, "I hope you will go and be saved today. I have been praying for you. I'll be glad to walk down with you to tell the preacher that you want to accept Christ as Saviour, and I'll help to show you how to make sure. Won't you come with me?" So with a kindly hand on this visitor's arm, he is encouraged to go forward to take Christ as Saviour.

But in the formal worship service he comes into a some-what darkened auditorium where a funeral quiet reigns. The organ plays something he does not know. No little children in the service! They are in the basement in a "junior church." If a child does whisper, he is hushed at once; not a whisper, not a handshake, not a greeting here. This is the house of God! The choir sings an anthem which of course the stranger, the unchurched man, never heard. The singing is not informal and folksy, like the song fest at the Kiwanis Club which he attended. When he marched as a soldier in the army they sang happy songs and he could understand the words, but not here! This is religious! The sermon is philosophical and cultural, and perhaps expounds the Scripture, but it does not appeal to his heart. There is no public invitation to accept Christ, and if there were one, no one would feel free to come and speak to him or offer to go with him to the front to claim Christ. The choir is in robes: his wife likes to sing but he supposes they wouldn't want her in this special crowd of professional singers.

I say, there is no freedom in the formal service for soul winning.

Some good churches, some evangelistic churches, have robed choirs. But no one ever leaves the choir in his robes to walk down the aisle to a sinner friend and urge him to come to Christ. No, the robe puts a stop to that.

The formal service curbs the music leader. The song service cannot be bright, informal, evangelistic. It curbs the preacher and hinders the red-hot evangelistic appeal. It limits the freedom of the people to meet a stranger, and more than that, limits the personal work among the audience by those who want to see sinners saved.

III. Formalism in Church Services Is Directed Not to God but the Natural Man, Not the Spiritual Man

I believe that God is the author of all things beautiful in

nature: beautiful scenery, beautiful color, the beauty of exact mathematics, the beauty of intricate chemical formulas, the beauty of music, the rainbow, the mountains, the sunset, the seashore--all these, I think, are of God. But we should remember that while nature reminds us of the Creator, it does not show the plan of salvation and does not make Christians. That has to come through divine revelation, the Bible. Those who defend formalism in the churches speak of "a spirit of reverence" and a "worshipful attitude." But they ought to remember that heathen people are often reverent and awed, and an infidel may love beautiful scenery or a symphony orchestra or a sunset. Just so millions of unconverted religious people take part in church ceremonies. Unconverted priests intone Latin phrases, conduct a mass, say prayers. I say, one of the most beautiful prayers I have ever read is the prayer of general confession of the Episcopal church. Yet I have no doubt that multiplied thousands repeat that prayer each week who have never penitently turned from their sins to trust in Jesus Christ.

It must be particularly offensive to God to have the organ playing during prayer or during what purports to be prayer. Jesus said, "Do not your alms before men, to be seen of them" as the hypocrites do, and "When thou prayest, thou shalt not be as the hypocrites are: for they love to pray standing in the synagogues and in the corners of the streets, that they may be seen of men." He said that those who fast and otherwise pretend to seek God's face, "that they may appear unto men to fast," are "as the hypocrites." Surely He must turn His face away in disgust at this which He has thrice called "hypocrisy." Men pretend to seek God when they pray, but actually they try to impress men.

Such people think it a virtue that they would musically deal with the cultured and aesthetic while they pretend to pray and thus provoke what they call "reverence." But they should still remember that they are really pointing the prayer toward men when they pretend to address God. The music is not to influence God but to influence men, and that is what Jesus particularly forbade and called hypocrisy!

And their so-called "reverence" which people thus seek to inculcate by ceremonies, beautiful language, beautiful music, colorful and impressive liturgy, is not a spiritual quality, but a cultural and aesthetic quality. They seek what an infidel really means when he says that he can worship God as well sitting by a shady stream with his pipe and fishing line, as in church. An unsaved man may enjoy a symphony orchestra, a beautiful sunset, or a poetic expression as much as a Christian. You see, organ during prayer appeals not to the spiritual nature but to the sensual, the carnal. And the fact that it is professedly religious does more harm than good. For the unconverted heart which salves its conscience with religious ceremonies is all the harder to reach and bring to repentance and faith and a new heart. Men enjoy pious and cultured forms when they ought to be repenting of their sins or pleading with the Saviour for souls. In such forms and ceremonies people do what Jesus most sadly rebuked. "Ye hypocrites, well did Esaias prophesy of you, saying, This people draweth nigh unto me with their mouth, and honoureth me with their lips; but their heart is far from me. But in vain they do worship me, teaching for doctrines the commandments of men" (Matt. 15:7-9). And we should not forget that the cultured and religious Pharisees also made much of religious ceremonies, and Jesus said of such, "Many will say to me in that day, Lord, Lord, have we not prophesied in thy name? and in thy name have cast out devils? and in thy name done many wonderful works? And then will I profess unto them, I never knew you: depart from me, ye that work iniquity" (Matt. 7:22, 23).

The deadly thing about formalism is it satisfies people with beauty instead of with God. It satisfies men with words, phrases, forms, ceremonies and rituals, who ought never to be satisfied without being born of the Spirit and being saved, ought never to be satisfied except with the simplicity of New Testament Christianity and with the one great aim of soul winning.

It is sadly true that the carnal heart would rather have the good works of men than the miraculous work of Christ. It would rather fit the Gospel to the rich than to the poor. But that monstrosity of Rome shows that formalism leads away from New Testament truth, away from New Testament morality, away from New Testament soul winning.

And if some reader would brush aside all the arguments I have brought, it still remains true that the formal church is not the soul-winning church. And one of the principal reasons our churches do not win souls is that they seek to please men with rites and ceremonies, beauty and culture, instead of returning to the passion, power and simplicity which New Testament Christians had.

8. Church Music Usually Does Not Tend to Soul Winning

Where are the songs of the great revivals? It is sadly true that now few songs are written with a gospel appeal to the unsaved or to the unchurched, or cold Christians. Once multitudes were moved with "Tell Mother I'll Be There." Billy Sunday, baseball player in Chicago, was sitting on a Chicago curb when he heard a group from the Pacific Garden Mission sing his mother's favorite, "Where Is My Wandering Boy Tonight?" He got up, followed them to the mission, and was saved.

What new song do you know like "Ye Must Be Born Again," like "For You I Am Praying," and like "The Great Judgment Morning," songs like those written by P. P. Bliss, Charlie Tillman, or E. O. Excell? Where are the songs on soul winning like "Must I Go, and Empty-Handed?" And "Will There Be Any Stars in My Crown?" What recent song challenges like "Is Thy Heart Right With God?" by Kilpatrick, and that sweet, old heart-moving "I've Wandered Far Away From God, Now I'm Coming Home"?

"The Old Rugged Cross" was copyrighted fifty-two years ago and in a half century since only two or three gospel songs that I know of have been taken into the hearts of Christian people everywhere. Perhaps "He Lives" and B. B. McKinney's sweet invitation song, "Wherever He Leads I'll Go," and that popular gospel song, "How Great Thou Art," are the exceptions. When there are no great revivals and no great evangelistic preaching, then song writers do not write evangelistic songs. And the music of our churches does not emphasize soul winning and usually does not fit into a soul-winning program.

Dr. Jack Hyles says, "Evangelism is not a building, not

only the preaching. Evangelism is an atmosphere. Warm, fervent gospel music is part of the atmosphere. In a service with anthems and formal hymns the preacher and the people are tranquilized before the sermon, instead of being aroused, inspired, charged for soul winning. The music must make an atmosphere for soul winning."

I. Often the Music Does Not Attract or Bless Common People

In formal services the choir will sing an anthem. Allow me to be a musical heretic now and say that most of the anthems are ordinary and poor, musically. They are generally correct but uninspired. They meet certain mechanical standards of the musician, but they do not move hearts. How strange that music directors and pastors should think it wise to train a choir to sing an anthem, which may not be sung again for a year or for five years, or never. No one requests it again; no one is blessed by it. The strains do not linger in the heart. The message leads no one to repentance or to the joy of salvation. The words may be scriptural and devotional, but they usually are not evangelistic.

And the sad part is that the music of most anthems is not interesting to common people. It is not catchy, does not attract the ear with rhythm or melody. The lyric does not have rhyme and meter and simplicity to make it stick to the heart. Not only does such music fail to interest common, ordinary people everywhere, but it leaves the impression that Christianity is more or less a routine matter, not very attractive; all right for those who want it but of no special help to the common man.

Then the more formal the service, the more the gospel songs are eliminated and old hymns used. Now there are many old hymns and in some of them I delight. But it is also true that many of them, while sound in doctrine and correct as literature, are not specially musically attractive. Even the sentiment of many of the hymns may provide a devotional inspiration for Christians, but have no special appeal to children and lost people.

The sad truth is that the music of our churches has been largely taken over by unspiritual people, and the constant pressure is to do away with the gospel songs, do away with the evangelistic emphasis.

In Christian magazines even of fundamental and orthodox standards it is the usual thing to have an article decrying rhythm in gospel songs as if rhythm were itself evil. It is sometimes called "the beat of the jungle." We are reminded that in the dance halls the music has rhythm and therefore, foresooth, there ought to be no rhythm in the house of God! The simple truth is that rhythm is a God-given ingredient of good music, and there is no music without it. And the more the rhythm is subdued, the more difficult is the music and the less musical!

General Booth, who founded the Salvation Army, learned long ago that the churches were not reaching the common people, and one reason was the stilted, formal stylized music in the churches. So he took music hall tunes and had gospel words written to them. He had the music played on street corners with brass bands and with common people singing. Rhythm attracts people in gospel songs just as rhythm attracts people in the dance hall or the night club. Rhythm may be perverted, and so may the other essentials of good music be perverted, but rhythm is not wrong and to play down this beautiful element in music is a way to make the church music unattractive and dull, not helpful to the Christian and not affecting lost sinners.

The advocates of formal music in the churches often speak scornfully of "syncopation," as if it were an evil. Some worldly music is syncopated, and so, they argue the Lord's music should not be! I am sorry to believe that usually such men write out of musical ignorance as well as out of spiritual lack of perception. The musical device of syncopation is legitimate, and often brightens a tune.

I am reminded of an interesting and happy incident here. Some years ago Robert H. Coleman was the principal music publisher among Southern Baptists, and his songbooks, reputable and good, were widely used in hundreds of thousands of copies, particularly among Southern Baptists. Once when a new song came out (in 1914), he heard it and liked it very much. It was so bright it quickly became popular, but the syncopated tune was so lively and alluring--would his pastor like it?

Robert H. Coleman was assistant pastor and song leader of the First Baptist Church in Dallas, the largest church in the world, where Dr. George W. Truett was pastor. Dr. Truett was away on a speaking tour. The new book was getting ready for the press. With fear and trembling, Mr. Coleman included the new song.

Dr. Truett returned. The question of the new songbook came up and Dr. Truett said, "Bob, I don't often suggest, but I heard a song in the North by Charles H. Gabriel that I hope you can include in the new songbook. How thrilling it was! It is "Since Jesus Came Into My Heart." Gladly Mr. Coleman told his pastor that he had already selected that song. And the song, because of its syncopation and its lilt has been a blessing to millions, was included in spite of those who criticize syncopation and rhythm in gospel songs!

Do not misunderstand me. There is a place for great music in the churches. In the Galilean Baptist Church of Dallas, which I pastored seven and a half years, I had my eighty-voice choir prepare and give the Hallelujah Chorus. Later I had song leader Strat Shufelt train the three hundred voices in our city-wide campaign in Buffalo to give the Hallelujah Chorus and present it there. But in each case I played it up, I got people to expecting it, I taught them the beauty of it, and it was used as an evangelistic asset. I love "Unfold Ye Portals" and "The Palms" and "The Holy City." Long ago I learned the beauty of fine secular music: The Sextet from Lucia, the Strauss waltzes, Langes Flower

Song, Barcarolle, The Anvil Chorus, and others. In the university I sang as one of four hundred voices presenting "St. Matthew's Passion" by Bach. But the simplest song in the world, be it only folk music, country music in melody, and doggerel in words, if it reaches the hearts of people and is most used to turn men to Christ, is better than the finest which is not so blessed of God.

Unfortunately church musicians are usually more concerned with culture than with evangelism. They are trying harder to raise the musical standards of the congregations than to win men to Christ. So the music often does not interest and does not affect the mass of common people, nor attract them to the churches.

Dr. Jack Hyles says, "If you want Billy Sunday results, you must have Homer Rodeheaver music. If you want Moody and Torrey revivals, you must have Sankey and Alexander music."

II. Musical Instruments Traditionally Are Not Used to Best Advantage for Soul Winning

Musical instruments were used in the praise of God in Old Testament times. Second Samuel 6:5 tells us, "And David and all the house of Israel played before the Lord on all manner of instruments made of fir wood, even on harps, and on psalteries, and on timbrels, and on cornets, and on cymbals." And I Chronicles 15:28 takes pains to mention the same instruments about the same event. In the blessed revival under Hezekiah, "...He set the Levites in the house of the Lord with cymbals, with psalteries, and with harps, according to the commandment of David, and of Gad the king's seer, and Nathan the prophet: for so was the commandment of the Lord by his prophets" (II Chron. 29:25). And Paul the apostle, reminding the Corinthians that they were not to use foreign languages in the services, languages which could not be understood, said, "And even things without life giving sound, whether pipe or harp, except they give a distinction in the sounds, how shall it be known what is piped or harped?" (I Cor. 14:7).

There was no set formal pattern to services in New Testament churches as far as we know, and we think that, to keep it so, God did not order musical instruments to be used regularly in the services since poor congregations would have none. Yet it may be fairly inferred that there were pipes and harps sometimes used in the music of the churches, and they are not mentioned unfavorably in the discussion of public services.

Musical instruments have a place in the services of praise, and may be used of the Spirit of God for great spiritual blessings. When Saul became desperately melancholy, he had David come to play for him. "And it came to pass, when the evil spirit from God was upon Saul, that David took an harp, and played with his hand: so Saul was refreshed, and was well, and the evil spirit departed from him" (I Sam. 16:23).

Since God was with David, we think the Holy Spirit used his music to quiet the tormented mind of Saul. When Elisha was called on to intercede with God and find rescue for the armies of Israel and Judah, about to be destroyed, he said, "But now bring me a minstrel. And it came to pass, when the minstrel played, that the hand of the Lord came upon him" (II Kings 3:15), and he had God's miraculous answer.

So musical instruments can be used by the Spirit of God. However, there are certain limitations imposed by tradition which often hinder the soul-winning use of instruments and music in the house of God.

1. The Traditions for the Organ in Church Fit Formalism, Liturgy, Modernism, Not in Evangelistic Service

The pipe organ was tremendously expensive and might cost from $20,000 to $100,000 which compared with the piano in the old days at $250 to $500. So the organ was for the elite, for the wealthy church. Ordinarily the organist was paid and so was usually a professional musician, often not a Christian, sometimes very worldly. Churches, proud of their organ, would have organ prelude and postlude. So in honor to culture and prestige, it became customary to demand quiet "reverence" during the playing of the organ. Professional organists are a very proud and independent people, so usually they selected the music to be played and often selected the hymns. And if a church must invest so much in its music, then the more well-to-do churches had paid soloists, paid quartets, and sometimes even paid choirs. Professionalized music may tend to culture, but it does not tend toward soul winning. The tradition of the organ is not the tradition and background of evangelism.

Moreover, the organ had a background of the great cathedrals and the liturgical churches in Europe and England. So with the organ to many people and churches came the flavor of a divided chancel, the robed priest or choir, classical music instead of gospel music.

Moreover, the pipe organ is not a percussion instrument. The air blowing into one giant tube and then another does not make the instant staccato beginning of a tone as does the piano. The piano key hits sharply and strongly, exactly on the beat. The organ tone swells to its maximum a little later. So the pipe organ does not emphasize rhythm as clearly as the piano, and so does not help the congregation to keep the beat, and the pipe organ is not so instantly versatile to follow the leader. Singing with a pipe organ, the congregation usually sings with the organ, and the organ sets the pace and goes strictly according to the music, with little room for varied interpretation. With the piano, people and piano follow a leader. With the organ, they follow principally the organ and the organist. Or if there is a leader with the organ, then the leading is more or less routine. The electric organ is more versatile than the pipe organ, but still there is a tradition connected with organs that is not specially favorable to soul winning.

For music that contributes to soul winning, music that

reaches the mass of common people and moves their hearts, attracts the unsaved, and urges them toward decision, we think of Charlie Alexander with a tremendous choir in the Torrey meetings and Robert Harkness at the grand piano, or the team is Homer Rodeheaver and pianist Ackley in the Billy Sunday campaigns.

The formal churches are slow to use the piano. In one great First Baptist Church with which I am familiar, the piano was never used on Sunday morning, only Sunday night. The piano was all right for young people or for an informal service, but did not carry the prestige and formality inherent in the use of the organ, it was felt.

2. Other Instruments Usually Not Used to Beautify Church Music

Churches are slow to use an orchestra. If there be an orchestra, it may be used Sunday night, not Sunday morning.

In recent years the cornet and trombone are sometimes used for special numbers, but rarely in connection with congregational singing. Why not? Some Scandinavian churches with evangelistic bent used to have stringed bands. They were popular and very sweet, a great help, and made the music very attractive.

In the great Chicago Tabernacle Paul Rader had a tremendous band that played regularly in my meetings there in May, 1930, and was a great attraction.

The Salvation Army has long known the value of a brass band and drum to help get a crowd in street meetings and to use in the Army meetings.

If instruments of beautiful music have added greatly to the beauty and charm of singing Caruso, Madame Schumann-Heink, Mario Lanza, Perry Como, Kate Smith or Bing Crosby, why should they not be used to enrich, sweeten and help carry the message of gospel solos, duets and choir numbers? And if the combination of many instruments is wonderfully attractive in the night club and theatre, why should not these attractions be consecrated to God? Does an instrument of beautiful music belong to the Devil, or is God Himself the Author of all beauty? And why are the rhythmic chords of the guitar or banjo not suitable for praising God? They bring great enjoyment to common people everywhere and we believe they ought to be used widely in the Lord's service.

3. Special Music Does Not Usually Move the Heart

There is a clear command in the Bible that those who sing the songs of the Lord should be filled with the Spirit. Ephesians 5:18, 19 says, "And be not drunk with wine, wherein is excess; but be filled with the Spirit; Speaking to yourselves in psalms and hymns and spiritual songs, singing and making melody in your heart to the Lord." And Colossians 3:16 admonishes, "Let the word of Christ dwell in you richly in all wisdom; teaching and admonishing one another in psalms and hymns and spiritual songs, singing with grace in your hearts to the Lord."

So our songs ought to have a scriptural message, and ought to be sung in the power of the Spirit and with the special grace of God on the singer.

Thus the principal requirement of those who sing for the Lord ought not to be natural talent, nor musical training, but the moving of the Spirit of God upon them! God may use talent if it be consecrated and dedicated and has the breath of God upon it, but the talent, the training is not first even in secular music. A Harry Lauder or an Al Jolson may sing to more people than a Caruso. Although the voices of these entertainers were only ordinary, the spirit and personality and interpretation with which they sang were more important. And, surely, in singing for God, a moving of the heart by the Holy Spirit and a heartfelt expression of gospel truth is far more important than talent and training and musical prestige.

But the freedom of the Spirit in singing demands a certain freedom and informality in singing, as it does in preaching.

It is not surprising if one stands to witness for Christ, talks to an unsaved loved one or friend and is greatly moved and weeps. The Spirit-filled preacher does not like to be hampered by a robe, and he may laugh or sing or weep or pound the pulpit or gesture. Why should the soloist in religious service stand like a statue with impassive face and hardly recognizable words when she sings?

"The children of this world are...wiser than the children of light," Jesus said. So the grand opera singer gestures and manifests joy, or rage, or love, with facial expression and movement. Mary Garden was not the best singer, but was immensely popular in grand opera because she was a great actress, a great performer when she sang. Though the popular singers in the secular and entertainment world may sing doggerel or beautifully poetic lyrics, yet they must feel and express in face and hands and movement what the songs mean. The successful entertainers are not necessarily those with great voices.

Does anyone think the ancient Sophie Tucker or big-nosed Jimmy Durante have great voices? Enthusiasm, personality and interpretation make them greatly loved. Kate Smith and Perry Como, with sweet, lovely voices, win more by their charm than their voices. Why cannot Christian singers go all-out to move and bless, as secular singers do to entertain?

It has been my very great privilege as an evangelist to have associated with me from time to time many of the best-known and the most-used gospel singers of our time-- Homer Rodeheaver, Dr. Harry Clarke, Strat Shufelt, B. B. McKinney, Herbert Tovey, and Bill Harvey among them. And those most used and blessed both in the song leading and solo work are those with the most freedom of the Spirit, those who with whole-souled concern and enjoyment, sing to move and bless the people.

No preacher of the Gospel should preach just simply as routine "worship," without intending to impress upon Christians certain duties, certain changes needed. Why should musicians be purposeless or powerless or unmoving?

Psalm 47:1 says, "O clap your hands, all ye people; shout unto God with the voice of triumph." Again verses 6 and 7 say, "Sing praises to God, sing praises: sing praises unto our King, sing praises. For God is the King of all the earth: sing ye praises with understanding."

It is true that some would be shocked if God's people clapped their hands in time to the music in a service where hearts were deeply moved. But that would not necessarily displease God. Psalm 35:27 says, "Let them shout for joy, and be glad, that favour my righteous cause; yea, let them say continually, Let the Lord be magnified, which hath pleasure in the prosperity of his servant." Shouting for joy is not out of order if it comes from the heart in any time of praise. The Holy Spirit says in Psalm 33:1-3, "Rejoice in the Lord, O ye righteous: for praise is comely for the upright. Praise the Lord with harp: sing unto him with the psaltery and an instrument of ten strings. Sing unto him a new song; play skilfully with a loud noise."

Christian singing should be rejoicing. It should be with heart praise. It should be accompanied with harp and psaltery and other instruments. It ought to sometimes be with a loud noise as well as skilfully.

You may be offended if in a Pentecostal service people lift up their hands in exultation when they sing, but Psalm 63:3, 4 says, "Because thy lovingkindness is better than life, my lips shall praise thee. Thus will I bless thee while I live: I will lift up my hands in thy name." You may be sure that God is not displeased and common people are not unmoved when with great exultation of heart people show their joy in their singing, in their attitudes. You with austere traditions of formalism may not like the finger-snapping male quartets, nor the informality of guitar-playing soloists, but these people, often with untrained voices, regularly fill the largest auditoriums in towns for all-night sings! And some people drive fifty miles to stay up all night and hear such singing! Now try to draw such crowds and hold them and bless them with pipe organ and anthems! Informality and heart fervor in the music will serve God better than formal training and natural talent without the breath of Heaven and the freedom of the Spirit.

Our songs say much about shouts of praise. They frequently have the term, "Hallelujah." But with uninspired singing we rarely hear a heartfelt hallelujah.

Sometime ago, in a great convention of soul winners, a trio sang very beautifully of Heaven. Dr. Harold Sightler of the large Tabernacle Baptist Church, Greenville, South Carolina, was to speak. The pastor who introduced him said, "If that quartet had been singing in Dr. Sightler's church they would have had trouble finishing because of the shouting." When Dr. Sightler rose to speak he said, "Yes, people do often praise the Lord aloud in our services, but shouting is not all we do." And he told about the tens of thousands of dollars sent annually to mission work, the multitudes saved, the orphan children cared for, and then he said, "Driving here today, I heard the Moody Chorale sing the wonderful "Hallelujah Chorus" by Handel, and I thought: They can sing, 'Hallelujah,' but if somebody said it in a service, they might faint!"

Don't you think that a heart attitude ought to match the music more, and heart praises ought to be expressed in face and interpretation? And the pleading of an invitation song ought to be Spirit-filled pleading.

Sadly, our churches do not have music that is Spirit-filled and reaches the heart, so usually is little help to soul winning.

9. The Sunday School Is Usually Not Utilized Fully in Soul Winning

A pastor sat in his study throughout the Sunday school session. He confided in me that he was so concerned about his sermon that he never took any part in the Sunday school. He must save his best thought and efforts for the Sunday morning "worship service." He taught no classes. He attended none of the assemblies of the Sunday school. He took no responsibility for the Sunday school. Obviously, he was not helping the church to use the Sunday school as a great soul-winning and enlistment agency.

Why, I have known of Sunday schools where the teachers were not even members of the local church and where the superintendent never even stayed for the morning church service! And, of course, many of the teachers and many of the pupils did not stay. I find in many Sunday schools the church does not elect the officers and teachers, does not even pay for the Sunday school literature. And in many Sunday schools, the Sunday school not only takes its own offerings and pays for its own literature, but it selects the literature, elects the teachers, and sometimes has its own mission program like a separate church!

Even in the churches that are better organized and more efficient, often the Sunday school must compete with some or all of the following: Women's Missionary Society, Training Union, Epworth League, Royal Ambassadors, Girls' Auxiliary, Young Women's Auxiliary, or laymen's meeting.

Thousands of good churches make much of the Sunday school, yet speak of the Sunday school as simply "the teaching service of the church," and do not make adequate use of the Sunday school organization for soul winning and enlistment.

I. Sunday School Is Church's Greatest Opportunity

Other organizations may try to reach the women, or the men, or the young people, or children of various ages, or the choir, but the Sunday school is the one church organization that should have contact with all the church membership and the church families, and should be the greatest outreach for soul winning and enlistment.

1. Sunday School Offers Best Opportunity to Reach Children and Young People

The Sunday school ought to reach not only the children, but certainly it is the best opportunity to reach children for Christ. Even the poorest Sunday schools have children, the children of the regular attending families of the church, and some others.

Dr. Jack Hyles of the First Baptist Church of Hammond, Indiana, tells how, as a little barefooted boy, he went to Sunday school in the primary department and a lovely Christian teacher took him on her lap, made him feel at home, told him that God loved him. When he asked the teacher if God loved him as much as other little boys and girls who had nice clothes and shoes, she told him, "Yes, Jackie, I expect He loves you more." The boy never got away from that influence. Later he turned to Christ.

Dr. Lee Roberson tells how, as a high school boy, he was invited and attended a Sunday school class, how the teacher went faithfully and carefully over the plan of salvation. He did not stay for the preaching service. Again he went to the Sunday school class, and again she went faithfully over the plan of salvation, urging each one to trust the Saviour. He did, and stayed for the preaching service and claimed the Lord. No wonder he now stresses a great home Sunday school and many chapels, reaching sometimes 4,500 in total Sunday attendance, and uses these Sunday schools as a soul-winning and enlistment agency.

D. L. Moody attended a Sunday school in Boston, an orphaned seventeen-year-old boy. The Sunday school teacher sought him out in the shoe store where he worked and won him to Christ. Small wonder that D. L. Moody began his ministry, first as a Sunday school teacher, with a ragged boys class that he recruited from the streets, and, then, at his own Sunday school which grew to be the largest of his day, so that even President Abraham Lincoln visited it in Chicago. That Sunday school grew into the now famous Moody Memorial Church. And Moody started his great soul-winning work outside his own city, primarily in Sunday school conventions where he taught people how to have a soul-winning Sunday school and set the revival fires burning and won many himself.

In large congregations all over America, when put to the solemn public test, I have found that more than half of all the people who claimed to be converted in congregations north and south, east and west, and in Canada, claimed to have been saved before they were fifteen years old! If they are not saved as children, most people will never be saved.

The late Dr. H. A. Ironside, for eighteen years pastor of the great Moody Memorial Church in Chicago, tells how he learned the same truth:

> I shall never forget listening night after night to Dwight L. Moody in the old Hazzard's Pavilion, Los Angeles, when I was but a lad of twelve. I could not get a seat the first night I went, the place was so full, so I climbed out on one of the steel girders reaching from the top gallery supported from the roof, and there I lay looking down upon the great throng, watching the sturdily-built matter-of-fact business-like man, who had been advertised as the renowned evangelist, Moody. I was greatly impressed by his intensity, and many a time as I lay there, I said in my heart, "Oh, how glad I would be if I could someday reach great throngs of people with the Gospel in the way that man is doing."
>
> I remember so well one night Mr. Moody asked all who were sure they were converted to stand on their feet. He

kept them standing while the ushers gave an estimate of the number who had risen. They were reported to be between five and six thousand. Then Mr. Moody asked all who had come to Christ before they were fifteen years of age to sit down. To my amazement, fully two-thirds of that great throng dropped to their seats. Then he said, "All who became Christians before you were twenty, sit down." Less than one-half of those left standing remained on their feet. Then he requested all who were saved under thirty to sit down, and another great company took their seats. So it went on, those under forty, under fifty, and by that time there were perhaps not twenty people still standing. It was one of the most striking testimonies I have ever seen of the fact that the great majority of people are saved in early youth, and very few indeed ever turn to God after they have passed the one-half century.

The greatest harvest field in the world is among the children and young teen-agers, and the Sunday school is the best opportunity to reach these children and win them to Christ.

2. Sunday School Also the Greatest Opportunity to Reach Adults

Dr. G. Beauchamp Vick, pastor of the Temple Baptist Church in Detroit, one of the two or three largest churches in the world, has proved that the Sunday school is a great evangelistic agency for the whole church.

I preached for him one July Sunday, vacation season was on, and the Sunday school attendance was down. "The bottom dropped out," he said. I found that there were only something more than 3,800 present that July Sunday morning! (There have sometimes been over 5,000.) And Dr. Vick told me that the Sunday school attendance averaged fifty-eight per cent adults. Great departments of young married couples, departments for the middle ages, and departments for older people, sought out and invited and brought people to the house of God to hear the Word of God taught in the Sunday school.

That church regards the Sunday school as so important that they make that the one great organization of the church. The young people's department of the Sunday school may have a special service for young people before the Sunday evening preaching service, but there is no separate young people's organization, with separate officers and emphasis. All the missionary work of the church is emphasized through the Sunday school, and the Christmas offering for missions runs into many tens of thousands of dollars. So the visita - tion program, the soul winning, the enlistment in giving, is done through the Sunday school.

Recently Dr. Vick told me that they had received over 1,400 converts for baptism in the preceding year. Some of those were saved by visitation of Sunday school teachers and by workers from the adult classes. Some were saved in the classes. Others were brought from the classes into the morning preaching service and won to Christ. But the Sun - day school was the major organization agency that enlisted workers, trained the workers, who provide the workers in soul winning and enlistment.

3. Sunday School Can Make the Largest Impact on Whole Community for Soul Winning

The Bible command is that every church, every Christian, every group of Christians should go and preach the Gospel "to every creature" (Mark 16:15). If the church is to be ac - countable for getting the Gospel to every creature, then some organization like the Sunday school must be utilized. "Every person ought to win someone," is good counsel, but it won't work unless one works it. So the Christian may say, "Who should I win?" He might ask, "When shall I see him?" He might say, "What shall I say?" And so he needs to be taught and enlisted through the Sunday school to do the visiting. He may be given the prospects to visit; he may get his friends to come with him to the Sunday school class and then sit beside him in the auditorium to hear the Gospel. No church can have an adequate visiting and soul-winning program without some planning and organization for it. The Sunday school organization is the one to use.

The church has no other organization through which the whole community can be contacted.

II. Sunday School Should Be the Whole Church Organized for Evangelism

It is the work of the Sunday school to teach, yes! And the teacher is a teacher. But the teacher ought also to be a soul winner. He or she ought to be responsible to win the lost among the group that already attends. He ought to be responsible to enlist every other one available in that age and sex group and to win them to Christ.

1. Pastor Should Be Pastor of Sunday School

If the Sunday school is simply the whole church at work, then the pastor of the church should be pastor of the Sunday school. And since the Sunday school is the one principal organization that can reach the whole constituency, the pastor surely ought to be the pastor of the organization. There may be a superintendent. There may or may not be a paid full-time educational director, but the one most important figure in the Sunday school is the pastor. He has more influence with the people. He more nearly ought to be God's representative in the matter.

So the pastor ought to teach the church what a Sunday school should be. He should challenge the Sunday school teachers and officers in his preaching and in private counselling. He should conduct the teachers' meeting, or take certain specified responsibility in dealing with the teachers. He should be on the nominating committee which nominates the teachers. The pastors of most large soul-winning churches teach a large adult class. At any rate, the pastor should be pastor of the Sunday school and should largely color and influence the Sunday school organization and pro-gram.

In actual practice, in the most efficient and successful soul-winning churches, the pastor himself is Sunday school superintendent. Dr. Beauchamp Vick of Temple Baptist, Detroit, and Dr. Jack Hyles of First Baptist, Hammond, are actually officially superintendents of the Sunday school, while Dr. Lee Roberson of Chattanooga, and Dr. Tom Malone of Pontiac, Michigan, may have a layman "stand in" officially, but actually they supervise and administer the Sunday school.

2. Church Should Take Responsibility for Sunday School

I mean that if the Sunday school is the church at work and if the organization is simply the church organized for evangelism, then the church should elect the teachers. They should not be elected by the classes without the whole church acting on the matter. The superintendent and pastor and some others should make up a nominating committee. The preferences of adult classes should be considered, of course. But the teachers ought to be members of the local church. They ought to be born-again Christians, fervent in Spirit, true to the Word of God, clean in their lives. Besides that, a position is more important when it is by the election of the whole church. The church should elect the teachers and the superintendent.

Then the church ought to finance the Sunday school. Or to put it a better way, the Sunday school perhaps ought to be an agency in the church in teaching people to give, and offering envelopes ought to be provided in the Sunday school so that people can give to the whole church program, and have it recorded in the church office. Since the Sunday school is simply the church at work, then the church ought to be responsible for the expenses, ought to buy whatever literature and records are necessary, or pay whatever expenses of a teachers' luncheon at the teachers' meeting, or in buying awards for pupils, or whatever is needed.

The Sunday school officers are officers of the church. They ought to be the strongest Christians in the church.

3. Teachers Themselves Should Be Soul Winners

The teacher, in visiting absentees, in inviting new prospects, ought to win souls, and ought regularly to bring pupils into the preaching service and be ready to encourage them to claim Christ openly as Saviour. Whether the teacher wins a soul in the home or in the Sunday school class or brings them into the preaching service and there helps to get them to come to Christ, still the teacher is the great secret of soul winning in the Sunday school. So the church should train teachers to be soul winners and should elect people who are soul winners or who can be made into soul winners.

Of those who publicly claimed Christ last year at First Baptist Church, Hammond, 278 people were won to Christ by the Sunday school teachers. These teachers are taught how to win souls, and are required to report weekly how many visits each has made and how many souls have claimed Christ as results of their visits.

III. Methods of Soul Winning in the Sunday School

I have told you above how Dr. Lee Roberson was won to Christ in his Sunday school class and how D. L. Moody was won by his Sunday school teacher.

When I was an eight-year-old motherless boy, Mrs. Powers, my Sunday school teacher, said to us in the class with trembling lips, "I pray for all of you every day. I want you to be saved. I will never give you up. I will pray for you until the last one of you has been converted." I was deeply moved. If she had told me how, I think I would then have turned to Christ. Within a year, I suppose, I did find Christ as my Saviour.

But the influence of a good Sunday school teacher is almost beyond exaggeration. The group is small, her teaching is informal. She may ask questions or answer them. She may center on a particular pupil who needs the Lord. Thousands have been won to Christ in the Sunday school class.

1. Often a Whole Department Ought to Have an Evangelistic Service

In well-organized and departmentized Sunday schools, a number of classes of the same general age group meet together for opening exercises and perhaps for closing of the Sunday school. In effect that department is a separate little Sunday school, with its own department superintendent and its own opening and closing services. For example, in many Sunday schools, those whose ages are nine to twelve are in the Junior department, and that is the most fruitful age in which children are to be won to Christ, followed by the teen-agers from thirteen to seventeen, in another department. The departments may be called Junior High and High School Departments. In every Sunday school, at least once or twice a year there ought to be an earnest evangelistic appeal to the whole department in an effort to win to Christ the lost who are present. Sometimes it ought to be in the opening exercises. Other times it ought to allow the classes to assemble separately to complete their records, then come back to spend the Sunday school hour in one evangelistic service. That service would usually be conducted by the pastor or an evangelist or someone else who is a proven soul winner. If the Sunday school is small and does not meet by departments, then it might be well to have such an evangelistic service with those from nine to twelve and on up to seventeen at one time, and perhaps young people and adults together at another time. At any rate, such an evangelistic service ought to have such a place of prominence, ought to be so carefully prepared and prayed over, that God can use it to save many souls. Teachers should have in mind those who are saved and those who are lost, and these records should be available. There should be detailed prayer, and a definite effort to win to Christ all the unsaved in the department.

Once I was asked to have such a service with some three hundred Junior boys and girls, ages nine to twelve, in the First Baptist Church of Fort Worth, Texas. Many were saved. One of those twelve-year-old boys was called Scotty because his last name was Scott. That summer he drowned in the Forest Park pool. The father, though of another faith, insisted I preach Scotty's funeral because I had won Scotty to Christ in that decision day in the Junior department. Following the funeral the whole family was revolutionized.

Oh, do not let them get away! Use the Sunday school department as an opportunity for soul winning.

2. Some Sunday Schools Have "Decision Day" Once a Year

For such a "Decision Day" there may be earnest prayer again and again for weeks ahead of time in the meeting of teachers and officers, and privately by the teachers themselves and other saved people. Then on "Decision Day," if there is no general meeting of the whole Sunday school, each department can have its own "Decision Day." In smaller Sunday schools where there is one general meeting, the period can be turned over to soul-winning time. Take care that the appeal is first made primarily to teen-agers and Juniors. Some Primary children can be won to Christ, but they ought not be put in the front to dominate the interest, and they ought to be encouraged to wait until you deal with older people. Soul winning of the more mature pupils ought to come first, then with some restraint younger children might have an opportunity to claim the Lord. One can properly put more pressure, more fervent entreaty in an appeal to a teen-ager who knows that he is lost and knows how to be saved, than would be proper to a group of smaller children who would be anxious to please the teacher or the pastor and might move before clearly understanding what was involved, if they are under too much pressure to act publicly.

"Decision Day" should deal primarily with those in the Junior department and above. Primary children can be won to Christ best in their own classes and department, and they ought to be won in the meeting of Primary children or personal dealing by teachers.

3. But the Teacher Has the Best Opportunity to Win Pupils and Others Personally

In more than forty years as an evangelist, with hundreds of campaigns and many thousands saved, it has been a blessed and oft-recurring sight to see a Sunday school teacher win a boy or girl who was in his or her class in Sunday school, but now present in the revival service. How often I have seen the teacher at the invitation suggest that the child come to Christ now, come to the front with the teacher, to tell the preacher and claim Christ openly. Sometimes the pupil was won as the teacher visited in the home. Other times he was won as the teacher most earnestly went to him quietly at the invitation time and while people sang softly, offered to come with the child to the front to make sure of salvation or to personally claim the Saviour after trusting Christ in the pew.

In a blessed united campaign in Huntington, West Virginia, with some thirteen churches, we had a Sunday school night and a set of $25 worth of books was offered free to the Sunday school library of any Sunday school that had at least seventy-five per cent of its enrollment present. We had a good deal of rivalry. The Sunday school of one small church in a poor section of town was able to bring a great crowd and seat them in a reserved section near the front. Any who would come to sit with their friends in the Sunday school section of their neighborhood church were welcomed. One teacher of an adult class was able to bring many lost men, and that night ten men came out of the one class to claim

Christ openly, all through the influence of the local Sunday school.

I have found that to have a big "Sunday School Night" on Monday night where you enlist all Sunday school officers and teachers to work at it, secures the largest crowd of the week, a better crowd even than Sunday night. In such a service we have the largest proportion of unsaved people present and frequently the largest number of professions of faith of any night during the campaign.

D. L. Moody had a wonderful experience in seeing a Sunday school teacher win the lost ones of his class to Christ. It caused Moody to give up his business career and enter full-time service. Here is the story in his own words, taken from Moody Still Lives, written by his son-in-law, A. P. Fitt:

> I had never lost sight of Jesus Christ since the first time I met Him in the store at Boston, but for years I really believed that I could not work for God. No one had ever asked me to do anything.
>
> When I went to Chicago I hired four pews in a church, and used to go out on the street and pick up young men and fill these pews. I never spoke to those young men about their souls: that was the work of the elders, I thought. After working for some time like that, I started a mission Sabbath School. I thought numbers were everything, and so I worked for numbers. When the attendance ran below one thousand it troubled me, and when it ran to twelve or fifteen hundred I was elated. Still none were converted, there was no harvest.
>
> Then God opened my eyes.
>
> There was a class of young ladies in the school who were without exception the most frivolous set of girls I ever met. One Sunday the teacher was ill, and I took that class. They laughed in my face, and I felt like opening the door and telling them all to get out and never come back.

That week the teacher of the class came into the store where I worked. He was pale, and looked ill.

"What is the trouble?" I asked.

"I have had another hemorrhage of my lungs. The doctor says I cannot live on Lake Michigan, so I am going to New York State. I suppose I am going home to die."

He seemed greatly troubled, and when I asked the reason he replied:

"Well, I have never led any of my class to Christ. I really believe I have done the girls more harm than good."

I had never heard anyone talk like that before, and it set me thinking. After awhile I said:

"Suppose you go and tell them how you feel! I will go with you in a carriage, if you want to go."

He consented, and we started out together. It was one of the best journeys I ever had on earth. We went to the house of one of the girls, called for her, and the teacher talked to her about her soul. There was no laughing then! Tears stood in her eyes before long. After he had explained the way of life he suggested that we have prayer. He asked me to pray. True, I had never done such a thing in my life as to pray God to convert a young lady there and then. But we prayed, and God answered our prayer.

We went to other houses. He would go upstairs, and be all out of breath, and he would tell the girls what he had come for. It wasn't long before they broke down and sought salvation.

When his strength gave out I took him back to his lodgings. The next day we went out again. At the end of ten days he came to the store with his face literally shining.

"Mr. Moody," he said, "the last one of my class has yielded herself to Christ!"

I tell you we had a time of rejoicing.

He had to leave the next night, so I called his class together that night for a prayer meeting, and there God kindled a fire in my soul that has never gone out. The height of my ambition had been to be a successful merchant, and if I had known that meeting was going to take that ambition out of me I might not have gone. But how many times I have thanked God since for that meeting!

The dying teacher sat in the midst of his class, and talked with them, and read the 14th chapter of John. We tried to sing "Blest Be the Tie That Binds," after which we knelt down to pray. I was just rising from my knees when one of the class began to pray for her dying teacher. Another prayed, and another, and before we rose the whole class had prayed. As I went out I said to myself:

"O God, let me die rather than lose the blessing I have received tonight!"

The next evening I went to the depot to say good-bye to that teacher. Just before the train started, one of the class came, and before long, without any prearrangement, they were all there. What a meeting that was! We tried to sing, but we broke down. The last we saw of that dying teacher he was standing on the platform of the rear car, his finger pointing upward, telling us to meet him in Heaven.

I didn't know what this was going to cost me. I was disqualified for business: it had become distasteful to me. I had got a taste of another world, and cared no more for making money. For some days after the greatest struggle of my life took place. Should I give up business and give myself wholly to Christian work, or should I not? God helped me to decide aright, and I have never regretted my choice. Oh, the luxury of leading someone out of the darkness of this world into the glorious light and liberty of the Gospel!

Oh, Sunday school teacher, the young people in your class or the prospects that you could get into your class, have precious souls and you are made responsible for them and must answer to God! Churches do not win many souls if they do not have soul-winning Sunday school teachers.

IV. Most Churches Fail to Have a Strong Visitation Program Through the Sunday School

Many churches, many pastors, and many Sunday school teachers feel that their work is primarily to teach the Sunday school lesson for thirty or forty minutes Sunday morning. But that is far from true. Would a pastor be doing his duty just to preach on Sunday morning, with no announcements, no promotion, no visitation, no advertising? Certainly not. Neither has a Sunday school teacher done his job just by teaching. Has the Sunday school superintendent done his job just by presiding over opening exercises of the Sunday school, and perhaps securing substitute Sunday school teachers for those teachers absent? Certainly not! God's plan for Christians and churches is that we are to take the Gospel "to every creature."

1. Every Teacher Should Visit Every Absentee Each Week

Not just a phone call, not just a postcard, but a personal visit from the teacher! And if the teacher for a young people's or adult class has too many to look after all the visitation, then the class should be divided into sections, with a leader or chairman of each section who will be responsible to see that every absentee in his section is visited. I know that some Sunday school workers think a postcard or phone call is enough, but that is not the plan that builds the great Sunday schools of America. It takes more concern than that, more work than that.

If there are many absentees, it may seem at first that it is an impossible job. But visiting will help secure regular attendance, will cut down the number of absentees. And, teacher, you must account to God for those enrolled in your class--to get them saved, then to get them enlisted in the church and baptized, to teach them the Word, to teach them to tithe, to pray, to read the Bible, to win souls.

2. Then Every Sunday School Class Should Keep List of Prospects for Visiting

Those prospects for the Sunday school can be secured in several ways. One way is a census of the community, recording names, ages, address and spiritual status of every man, woman, and child in the whole area, with church membership or preference. Sometimes that can be done by one church; at other times it can be done by several churches co-operating.

Another way to secure prospects is to have visitors in every Sunday service of the church fill out cards, with names and addresses and ages, and other information.

Then often the members of a Sunday school class can give the names and addresses of others of the same age group or others in their families who are not regularly attending church somewhere else. But the prospect lists are no good unless they are used. A good Sunday school organization will turn in to the teacher a list of her absentees and a list of prospects for visitation every week.

Many of the best churches have a night when people meet together and receive the cards of prospects, each visitor to be assigned names in the same general area, so that they can be visited between 7:00 and 8:30 p.m.

3. Bus Routes Require Much Promotion, Repeated Visits

Since such a bus route will bring people for a number of classes, the visitation for the bus route must be planned and supervised by the Sunday school administration. Sometimes one or two together can call from house to house and make a date to pick up the children at an exact time on Sunday morning. And those who did not awake in time or were not dressed or could not come, ought to be visited regularly, after every absence, to maintain the regular group picked up by the bus each Sunday morning. Teachers may help in the visitation of their own absentees if the bus route is not too far away from the church.

4. Teachers Must Teach and Enlist Converts

But all the visitation and soul winning done by the teacher in the class or in the homes ought to be followed up by teaching on public profession of faith and baptism. Converts ought to be brought to the public preaching services, and the teacher ought to be ready to walk down the aisle with them as they come to tell the pastor that they have trusted Christ and want to confess Him openly. The soul winner's work is not done until the convert has made open profession of faith and has joined in with God's people, followed Christ in baptism, and becomes a regular attendant at Sunday school and the church services.

So you see, the work of a Sunday school teacher is far more than simply teaching the Sunday school lesson on Sunday morning.

V. Churches Without Bus Routes Limit the Area Evangelized

Many churches miss the opportunity of evangelizing a wide area because they do not use buses to bring people to the Sunday school and preaching services.

Remember that the Sunday school is not simply an organization to teach the Word of God to those who happen to come. It should be the whole church organized to evangelize a whole area and to get the Gospel "to every creature." And there are many people who can be reached by providing transportation to bring them to the Sunday school and Sunday morning preaching services, who would not come otherwise. Some are poor and do not have cars or other transportation. Some parents are unsaved or disinterested, and yet would be glad to have their children go on Sunday morning if someone would come by for them. Many are poor and do not feel welcome in the average church (and perhaps they are not), unless they are lovingly enlisted and transportation is provided.

The great Highland Park Baptist Church in Chattanooga rents some of the city buses for Sunday morning. Immediately someone will say that the church cannot afford to rent buses to bring people to church. But the happy and surprising fact is that those who are brought to church in the buses will give enough in the services to more than pay their way. Most churches buy buses and find it is a splendid investment in building up the attendance and making soul-winning results possible.

1. Hard Work of Visitation and Enlistment Builds Bus Route

There is no use to announce a bus to cover a certain ground until someone plans out the route, then goes to visit house to house all along the area to be covered, getting names and addresses of those who would like to come on a bus ride on Sunday morning. It takes patience and hard work, but usually children will be glad to have a bus ride free. It can be made very attractive with choruses, fellowship, and a conversation with a teacher, or a "bus pastor," whom they will greatly admire.

The bus should run the route ahead of time, see exactly what minute it will be at a certain house or corner. Sometime one must hastily help dress a child. Those who do not get ready one Sunday, must perhaps be seen during the week. But it can be done with hard work.

Dr. Jack Hyles tells me that the buses bring in over seven hundred to his Sunday school and Sunday morning preaching services regularly. Remember that if you have buses, someone must work to fill the buses. Someone must preside and keep order on the bus. Someone must see that children get off at the right places.

2. The Extreme Effort Will Bring Results

One Sunday school had hot chocolate and rolls served on the bus for every child. Many of the children's parents did not awake in time to provide breakfast, so the children could not come unless someone saw after that. And that made an

extra incentive for children to come. If all the responsibility is left on prospective pupils to seek out the bus or to be
ready on time, without someone enlisting, encouraging, and
repeatedly going after them, the route will fail. With work,
prayer, faith and God's blessing, it can succeed.

3. The Buses Must Stay for the Preaching Service

It is foolish to spend all the effort to get people out to the
Sunday school service, then not take the full advantage of
keeping them there for the church service. You may say
that the parents will not want them to come unless they can
be home immediately after Sunday school, but in most cases
they can be persuaded to let their children stay. And if it
is taken for granted that all stay for the preaching service
and if the buses will simply not make any exception, then
the pastor can plan for a definite time to close his sermon,
can leave time for public invitation, for dealing with converts, can see that the buses are promptly loaded after the
service. If the service has enough blessing in it, parents
and children will soon be glad to join that plan. Thus those
who are saved in the Sunday school hour can come out openly in the preaching service. Those who are unsaved can be
brought into the preaching service and there, most likely,
won to Christ. Those who have been converted can be taught
to present themselves for membership and baptism.

4. The Buses Must Often Cover a Wide Area Claimed by Other Churches

John Wesley said, "The world is my parish," and Jesus
said, "Go ye into all the world, and preach the gospel to every creature" (Mark 16:15). Then no pastor or church has
a right to allow a ministerial association or some agree-
ment between pastors to keep him from reaching every
creature possible with the Gospel.

If a man, woman, or child is a member or a regular attendant of some good Bible-believing, soul-winning church,
well and good. Of course the church ought not pull people

away from another good church. But if one is unsaved and is not a regular attendant of any other church, then every Christian of any church has the solemn duty to try to win that person to Christ and to enlist him in Christian service. If your bus goes into the area claimed by some other church, there will be criticism. But will you be more concerned about pleasing a pastor or church who jealously, like a dog in the proverbial manger, would keep you from winning people that they do not try to win, or will you be more concerned about pleasing the Lord Jesus Christ who commanded us to go after "every creature."

If one is nominally a member of a false cult, or a member of a liberal church where the Gospel is not preached, why should you not try to win such people to Christ.

Movement creates friction. Success creates jealousy. The chief priests in Jerusalem complained to Peter and John, "Ye have filled Jerusalem with your doctrine" (Acts 5:28). Well, it is the solemn duty of every church and its members, in any given location, to reach all the unsaved people possible, in every direction, and to win them to Christ and teach them the Word. There is nothing to indicate that the New Testament churches did not reach every strata of society in seeking the lost regularly.

5. The Great Soul-Winning Church Must Go After the Poor

It was said of the Lord Jesus, "The Spirit of the Lord is upon me, because he hath anointed me to preach the gospel to the poor..." (Luke 4:18).

In the great supper about which Jesus spoke, the servant was commanded, "Go out quickly into the streets and lanes of the city, and bring in hither the poor, and the maimed, and the halt, and the blind" (Luke 14:21). The politician who wants the most votes must go after poor people. The soul winner who wants to win the greatest number of souls must go after poor people. The Lord Jesus said, "Blessed be ye poor..." (Luke 6:20). Oh, if our churches are to succeed as the Lord Jesus wants us to succeed in soul winning, we must everywhere go after the poor and win them to Christ and to the churches.

A closing word. Some Sunday schools have a system: if a pupil misses a certain number of Sundays, he is marked off the roll. Thus teachers may leave a good impression on their records; they do not have records showing far more enrolled than their regular attendance. I beg you, do not do it. Don't give people up so easily!

Dr. Lee Roberson said, "Only three reasons ever cause us to mark a pupil off the roll. First, if he dies. Second, if he joins another church and starts regular attendance there. Third, if he moves out of the state. Otherwise, he is still on our rolls, and we still urgently try to bring him back to the Sunday school and to Christ.

10. Only All-Out Effort Can Match New Testament Soul Winning

We know that the Great Commission command of Christ is that we are to "go...into all the world, and preach the gospel to every creature" (Mark 16:15). Anything less than an effort to reach "every creature," every living being that we can get to with the Gospel, is less than the obedience which Christ requires.

Jesus gave the parable of the man who made a great supper and sent his servant, first to those who had already been bidden, and then he said, "Go out quickly into the streets and lanes of the city, and bring in hither the poor, and the maimed, and the halt, and the blind." Then when the servant reported there was more room, he said, "Go out into the highways and hedges, and compel them to come in, that my house may be filled" (Luke 14:21, 23). And in the similar parable of the king who made a marriage supper for his son, the wholesale, all-inclusive nature of God's requirement of us as soul winners is illustrated by the king's command after some had treated his servants spitefully and slew them and he had destroyed them: "Then saith he to his servants, The wedding is ready, but they which were bidden were not worthy. Go ye therefore into the highways, and as many as ye shall find, bid to the marriage" (Matt. 22:8, 9). No church is meeting the New Testament standard unless it goes after "as many as ye shall find" for Christ.

We know that the New Testament churches, for example, the church at Jerusalem, followed that command so literally that we are told, "Daily in the temple, and in every house, they ceased not to teach and preach Jesus Christ" (Acts 5:42). And so at Pentecost there were three thousand added.

A few days later, "the number of the men was about five thousand" (Acts 4:4); a few days later there were "multitudes both of men and women" (Acts 5:14).

There is in our poor carnal natures a tendency to drift from all-out obedience to nominal obedience, from red-hot enthusiasm and zeal to a lukewarm, halfhearted way of doing God's business. As a great old song says,

> Prone to wander, Lord, I feel it,
> Prone to leave the God I love.

Thus there is need again and again in the churches for a revival of zeal, a revival of soul-winning compassion, a revival of the power of God upon us.

There is no way for a church to win souls after the New Testament pattern and measure except by an all-out effort.

I. There Must Be Constant Teaching and Preaching to Put Soul Winning First

The preacher must constantly judge his preaching on the basis of the souls that he wins and the souls that he leads other Christians to win. In the resurrection time that will be the basis of blessing: "And they that be wise shall shine as the brightness of the firmament; and they that turn many to righteousness as the stars for ever and ever"(Dan. 12:3). That is the basis now on which there is rejoicing in the presence of the angels of God: "I say unto you, that likewise joy shall be in heaven over one sinner that repenteth, more than over ninety and nine just persons, which need no repentance" (Luke 15:7).

So the Sunday morning sermon should be planned with this in mind: "How can I win the greatest number of souls to Christ today?" The Sunday evening service should be planned with the same purpose, or perhaps: "How can I so lead my people to the Christian habits and Christian witness and the power of God so that they may win the most souls?" Even on Wednesday night, in the midweek service, and at the teachers' meeting, and at the devotional that the pastor may give before the Women's Missionary Society, or his talk at the Rotary Club, or at the youth meeting, the aim ought to be, "How can I win the most souls for Christ and get others to win the most souls for Christ?"

I know, as does every successful evangelist, that there is no having of great ingathering of souls without a blessed reviving of the saints. I know that Christians must be taught to win souls, must be brought to penitence of their sins, must learn to do daily witnessing, must seek and must have the mighty power of God if they are to be soul winners. So to get the greatest number of people saved, a preacher must inspire and help God remake Christians into soul winners.

In the great Highland Park Baptist Church in Chattanooga it is very impressive to strangers who come on Sunday morning to find a fervent message which, although it may be partly addressed to Christians, is also slanted toward the unsaved. Then there is a fervent invitation, and usually many come forward to claim Christ. Some of them are saved in the visitation during the week; some are saved in that service. Then there is the baptizing. In the Sunday evening services also, a fervent message, an appeal to sinners and some come to claim Christ, and those who have been approved and received on their profession of faith are baptized. Then on Wednesday night, surprisingly enough, with a crowd that may run from 1,500 up to 2,000, the pastor preaches again fervently, and the choir has special singing to move the heart. There is an invitation to claim Christ, and again it is customary for people to come forward to claim Christ and be saved and unite with the church. Dr. Roberson has just told me that four people came to confess Christ as Saviour and were baptized last Wednesday evening. One was a woman 78!

The preacher, to make an all-out soul-winning church, will have to see that the deepest spiritual life is for the soul winner. The most blessed, life-changing knowledge of the

Word comes only to the soul winner. The holy dedication of a life of separation from worldliness and sin comes most readily to the soul winner, for Jesus has promised, "Every branch in me that beareth not fruit he taketh away: and every branch that beareth fruit, he purgeth it, that it may bring forth more fruit" (John 15:2).

In similar fashion, the Sunday school services, the young people's meetings, the choir rehearsals and fellowship meetings, the Daily Vacation Bible School must all be measured by this: the first burden on the dear heart of our Saviour is to see people saved, keep people out of Hell. We will never be the kind of Christians He wants us to be until that becomes first with us so that our constant aim is to win souls and teach others to win souls and make the climate and the spirit and the organization conducive to soul winning.

So the officers of the church will be elected, first, because they are soul winners. The first deacons who were elected were "seven men of honest report, full of the Holy Ghost and wisdom, whom we may appoint over this business" (Acts 6:3). What wonderful soul winners were Stephen, Philip and these other deacons! Then the idea will be to set such a standard and keep on such a holy pressure that the church officers, deacons, trustees, elders, will all be mainly occupied with winning souls. In the services, anything that does not tend toward getting people saved or teaching others to win souls will be changed to make it fit the one thing dearest to God's heart.

II. Of Course Such a Church Will Have Special Evangelistic Services

In a church that patterns after the New Testament churches in spirit and method, there ought to be special evangelistic services besides those regular Sunday services of the church. Every church should have a revival and evangelistic campaign, preferably twice a year. Although the custom has grown to have only eight days of such meetings at a

time, fifteen days, including three Sundays, is far more effective. If adequate preparation is made and enough prospects are known, more people will be saved the second week
than the first. If the church does enough preliminary work,
does enough advertising and enough visitation, and if the
preacher has enough spiritual resources to go a third week,
there will be more people saved the third week, and a larger congregation than the second week. It may be that in a
small congregation, most of the prospects available and
with which the church is familiar, can be won in the first
week or ten days. But the more the church enlarges its concern and its efforts, the farther afield it goes to reach people for Christ, the more effective such a revival campaign
can be. And unless the outreach goes before the preaching
and includes the same passion and holy zeal that the preaching needs, there will not be many to reap.

But if enough people are invited and challenged, and if
enough Christians bring lost sinners in their cars and sit by
them in the services, and if the teachers make an all out-
and-out effort to reach every pupil and every prospect, then
there will be enough contacts and prospects to have a blessed soul-winning revival.

Then churches ought often to take some responsibility for
revival campaigns outside the immediate area of the church.
For example, when I was pastor for seven and a half years
of the Galilean Baptist Church in Dallas (which was organized out of a blessed independent open-air revival campaign
held in 1932), we had great outdoor campaigns in many
parts of that flourishing city. I just counted over in my
mind nine different locations where we went either with a
large tent or with seating in the mild southwestern open air
or in a rented building. We had strong evangelistic campaigns. It took lots of work building benches or hauling
benches and piano, putting up lights, getting city permits,
advertising with sometimes ten thousand handbills, sometimes twenty thousand handbills given out from house to

house by volunteer workers, and with some advertising in the daily newspapers, and house-to-house visiting. We did not hinder other churches. Literally hundreds of our converts went into other churches that were located in the area where we had revival campaigns. Sometimes they resented our coming, sometimes they were indifferent, sometimes they were glad. But we pleased Christ and won souls, hundreds of them, really thousands of them. We enlisted enough of our own people for a choir. We raised the money for the expenses. We taught and persuaded and had days of fasting and prayer or had nights of prayer. So God helped us to get enough co-operation, enough hard work, enough prayer and influence to win many, many souls.

III. Every Church Should Reach People in Parks, Hospitals, Rest Homes, Vacation Bible Schools

There ought to be preaching in every place that an open door can be found. For instance, in the pastorate mentioned above, we had a regular team to visit the Parkland Hospital, the Woodlawn Hospital with TB patients, and every week take the Gospel to all who would listen. Many were hungry-hearted, eager for the literature they brought. There were regular weekly reports of souls saved. Each week we had a service in the county jail. Usually the pastor preached, sometimes we did visiting in the jail besides preaching. Some Federal prisoners were there and sometimes several hundred prisoners would be within reach of my voice in the four stories of cells, reaching above me. Each Sunday afternoon during the summer and as much of the year as the weather would permit, we had open-air services in Marsalis Park by the zoo. Where the crowds went, we went. And we won some souls to Christ there. We made friends with others who came to the church and later found the Saviour. We were trying to take the Gospel to "every creature."

A blessed opportunity for soul winning is in a Daily Vacation Bible School. It is the most favorable time to reach children and even teen-agers, since school is out and parents are glad to get the youngsters out of the way for a season. There is a general feeling even on the part of Catholics and modernists and of false cults, that it is good for young people to go to a religious school. So children may be reached for the Daily Vacation Bible School who cannot be reached for regular attendance at Sunday school. And in the Daily Vacation Bible School you may use three or four hours a day, five days a week, to teach the Word of God. Then there will be a big closing service in the evening when the parents are usually invited and will usually come and where the Gospel may be preached.

It is good to have whatever handwork, memory work, storytelling, singing choruses, is necessary to hold the attention and build up the children and young people who are already saved, but the primary aim of Daily Vacation Bible School ought to be to win souls. In every department there will be many who can easily be reached for Christ--from the primary ages on up to the high school ages. And it is surprising that many a church can enlist as many children in the Daily Vacation Bible School in two weeks' time as the total enrollment of the Sunday school! With three or four hours a day, it is possible to do enough teaching and preaching to make a tremendous impact on boys and girls. By all means the Daily Vacation Bible School should be used to reach many souls for Christ. And surprisingly enough, it is often found that unsaved mothers can be enlisted to use their cars to bring children to and from the school, or can be used to bake cookies or make kool-aid or lemonade, or provide some prizes. And such mothers are often won to Christ in the Daily Vacation Bible School by an alert pastor or teacher.

It will take planning. It will take some money. It will take lots of promotion. It will take sacrificial effort on the part of God's good people, but many souls can be won to Christ in such a Bible school every year.

In nearly every community there are rest homes or old people's homes where one may go with the Gospel. Usually, people are there who are neglected, who are rarely visited by their children. They are old. They are lonely. Sometimes they are senile. Sometimes a few are bedfast. But nearly always they delight to have some good reading material. Such people enjoy the old songs. They will come to the lounge to hear somebody preach the Gospel. They will be especially delighted if people visit them in their rooms, bring them flowers or dainties or reading matter and love.

IV. Invent Occasions to Reach Lost People With the Gospel

There are dozens of schemes which Christians can consecrate to the Lord's service, in order to reach lost people. A Father-and-Son-Banquet in a rural church, which I visited a year ago, with a good dinner provided by the church and with some special music, brought men and boys for fifteen or twenty miles, and some fathers and sons were unsaved. Five claimed the Lord in that service, as I recall. Others were contacted and made friends with evangelical Christians who in their own little churches would never hear the saving Gospel.

A favorite device is to have a banquet for mothers and daughters. Every mother can bring her daughter. Every daughter can bring her mother. It is sweet and scriptural to use the ties of mother love and filial pride to bring people out to hear the Gospel. A nice dinner, some special music, a reasonable price for the dinner (or a meal furnished free by good women of the church) will bring many women to hear the Gospel who otherwise would not be in an evangelistic service. And it will bring many teen-age girls and young women to hear the Gospel under the most favorable circumstances. Of course, there ought to be plain gospel preaching or teaching, either by a godly woman or by the pastor. It is certainly legitimate for a woman to bring the Gospel to women, though she would not feel free to preach to a mixed congregation, and should not.

Or there can be a dinner honoring the high school football team. The team will come, so will their dads and mothers and coaches and sweethearts! High school or college coaches and administration authorities will usually co-operate. And it always ought to be understood that it is done in the name of Christ and there must always be reserved freedom to have plain gospel preaching.

Or there can be a picnic for the high school seniors, or a hayride in a great truck with proper chaperonage, and then with a weiner roast over the outdoor fire and special music and a gospel message. People would sit on the grass in the flickering firelight. Or the hayride can end at a nice home with plenty of room where refreshments and a gospel service can be provided.

If a preacher is always preaching the Gospel, always taking advantage of each opportunity to say a good word for Jesus, he will find he can be invited to a big family reunion picnic to preach the Gospel, as I have been more than once.

A few months ago we returned from a tour of Bible lands with sixty-five people. We have heard amazing stories since that time. By using pictures of Bethlehem, Jerusalem, the Garden of Gethsemane, the sight of Solomon's Temple, the Jordan River, the Sea of Galilee, the ruins of the temple at Capernaum, and other like pictures, they were thrilled to give the story of the Holy Land. Again and again they have been invited, tour members write me, to give these lectures in churches, in grade schools, in a high school, and before a Kiwanis Club, and in a family reunion. And they find that hearts are very tender and that such an occasion can be turned to an evangelistic opportunity.

Or sometimes one may use that beautiful Bob Jones University film, "Red Runs the River," to get a great crowd, then give a gospel invitation. Or the sermon film by my brother, Dr. Bill Rice, "The Danger Trail," or evangelistic sermons on moving pictures, perhaps including some of my own messages, or a message by Dr. H. A. Ironside; all these may be used to get a crowd and a good reason to get people to come who would not otherwise come to hear the Gospel. In every case, of course, there should be plenty of time for a plain gospel message and an earnest invitation to accept Christ. No films, no entertainment, no quartet or a chorus should ever be used as a substitute for the Gospel. They may very properly be used as a drawing card to get people out to hear the Gospel.

If pastors and their people get obsessed with a holy zeal for soul winning and if soul winning becomes to them the greatest single aim and business in the world, then our churches can become great soul-winning churches.

V. Funerals and Weddings Are Gospel Opportunities

Every pastor will have an open door to many tender hearts at funerals. He will need to be wise and loving, but he may be surprised to find that at funerals people expect a preacher to talk about Jesus Christ, about Heaven, and telling the plan of salvation comes naturally there.

It was my great privilege to be invited to preach the funeral sermon of P. B. Chenault of the large Walnut Street Baptist Church in Waterloo, Iowa. He was a dear friend. He had been engaged in revival services in the church of which I was the pastor. On his way back North he was killed in an automobile accident. I went to Waterloo, Iowa, with the body to preach the funeral sermon. Since it was, as I recall, the largest church in the state, and since he had a radio program with many hearers, the church auditorium, the main floor, the balcony and the basement, were filled with a total of some 1,800 people, we estimated. On the platform beside me was Dr. Will Houghton, president of Moody Bible Institute; Dr. Robert Ketcham, representative of the General Association of Regular Baptist Churches; and several missionaries and other beloved ministers. I said what I could to comfort loved ones, and gave proper honor to my beloved brother who was gone, but I preached the Gospel plainly and gave an invitation for people to then and there take Christ as Saviour and stand publicly to be seen. A missionary went to the basement to preside there in this part of the service over the crowd that listened over loud-speakers. Some twenty-five claimed Christ as Saviour in one of the most moving services I have ever attended. No one felt that the gospel invitation was out of place at the funeral of this dear man of God, himself a good soul winner, when he had gone to be with the Lord and his body lay in the casket before us.

I remember another occasion far different. As an evangelist living at Fort Worth, Texas, with a daily radio broadcast, I was invited to preach a funeral under sad circumstances. A young couple had married. The girl was not ready to settle down and take her place as wife and mother. God sent a little baby, but she did not want to stay at home and look after the little one. One night at 1:00 a.m. as she came down the steps from a dance hall on Hemphill and Magnolia Streets in Fort Worth with another man, her young husband met her at the foot of the stairs and stabbed her to death. Now I was called to preach the funeral.

What could I say? It was not sensible to say things that were untrue about a sad case. I simply said to the relatives, friends and acquaintances gathered in the funeral hall that the dead could not hear me and I must preach to the living. I preached that life is short at best, and death is certain for all. I preached that sinners must come to meet God and that Jesus Christ is the only hope for a sinner to have peace with God now and a home in Heaven hereafter. Then I had the congregation bow their heads in prayer. I prayed. I asked for those who wanted to be saved, who realized that they were sinners and would like to be remembered then and there in the prayer, to lift their hands. I promised to pray and I did pray that God would help them trust Christ just then, and take Him as Saviour and Lord.

Then I stood by the casket as the crowd filed by. A sister of the poor, wayward wife whose body was in the casket came and put her face on my shoulder and wept. "Oh, Brother Rice, she was not ready! She wasn't ready!" she said. As they came one by one, five different people stopped to tell me that they then and there would take Christ as Saviour. No one was offended, because what I did was in loving kindness and with genuine heartfelt sympathy for those in trouble, and with no abusive words about the poor, troubled young woman whose funeral we attended.

But broken hearts are often open hearts, and many, many souls have I seen saved either as I met with loved ones before the funeral, or as I counseled as others came by to see the body, or as we waited and talked tenderly around the open grave. Funerals are an open door for evangelism for the loving and Spirit-filled Christian.

Weddings, too, are a blessed evangelistic opportunity. Usually, it is not convenient nor proper to give a public invitation to come forward and claim the Lord at a wedding, of course. But every sensible pastor surely counsels ahead of time with the young couple who comes to be married. And there is usually a wedding rehearsal for a church wedding and a reception afterwards. Hearts are very tender at a wedding.

At the last wedding in which I officiated, I won two young people, a brother and sister of the bridegroom, at the wedding rehearsal as we talked informally to them, one at a time.

In Dallas, Texas, I had earnestly pleaded with God one early morning that I might win a soul that day. I was crowded with duties that could not be postponed, getting ready for a blessed revival campaign. At last, when the pressing duties of the day were done, I had not been able to win a single soul to Christ, nor had I much opportunity even to talk to sinners. As I thought rather sadly on this, the telephone rang. It was a young couple wanting to get married. The man had had to work late. They preferred an informal wedding at my home. Loved ones would come with them. Would I perform the marriage ceremony?

They came to my home and, of course, I talked with them earnestly in private. No, they were not divorced. No, they were not running away to get married. Loved ones were present, and their plans seemed well considered. I took them apart alone to talk with them. This was a holy alliance they were entering, and they were to make a covenant with each other and God that would bind them "till death do us part." It was expected that God would send children. They would bear each other's burdens, look after each other when they were sick, forgive each other their wrongs. How they would need Jesus Christ in the home! They were deeply concerned. They were openhearted and soon they were glad to admit their need for Christ and were ready to pray for forgiveness and both trusted Christ as Saviour. Then we had a happy wedding ceremony.

O preacher, if you cannot take Christ to a funeral home or to the wedding, why should you go? Oh, to make people soul-conscious! To get Christians to where it is their daily prayer that they may meet someone whom they can win to Christ. To have Christians so plan their week that a certain time is set apart for house-to-house visitation.

VI. Godly People May Commit Themselves to a Goal in Souls Won

In chapter 5 I have told how in Dallas, Texas, several of us set personal quotas as our aim for six months of intensive personal soul-winning effort, and told how a seamstress won more than 150 in six months and 360 the following year, of my wife winning about 101 and of others who won twenty-five and thirty each. They did far more than they would have done without prayerfully, earnestly setting a goal, each for himself and each consistently working to win the number of souls he felt led to undertake. Sometimes by setting a quota as the minimum number that a person or an entire church ought to see saved within a year's time helps to put soul winning first and to make soul-winning effort systematic and persistent, as it ought to be.

Oh, only an all-out effort can make our churches match the New Testament standards of soul winning.

VII. Pastor and Church Seek to Enter Into the Personal Lives of All the Community for Soul Winning

A church that wins souls after the New Testament pattern is to seek to get the Gospel to "every creature," and is to carry the Gospel as they did in Acts 5:42, "And daily in the temple, and in every house, they ceased not to teach and preach Jesus Christ." Therefore the pastor and people should carefully seek to make contact with every individual possible, to enter into their joys, to praise them for success and promotion, to comfort them in their sorrow, to say a word for Jesus Christ whenever a door or a heart is open and so let the church become known over a wide area as being full of love for the poor, for people in trouble, and a friend to every person who needs help.

So the pastor and a responsible, spiritual group of Christian leaders ought to be in constant touch with the newspaper editor, with the county judge or city judge, with the superintendent of schools and the principals of the schools.

Let us suppose that a teen-ager is arrested for vandalism, not his first offense. He is from a divorced home, his mother works. There is no one to look after him. His home has no authority and no blessing, nothing to hold him. It may seem that there is nothing to do but send him to a reform school. But many a county or city judge or judge of a juvenile court would be glad if some godly businessman would be a guarantor for the boy, buy him clothes so he will not be ashamed, take him to Sunday school and preaching services and see that he meets other fine young people, and in it all seek to win the boy to Christ. This Christian man can see that the young fellow reports each week to the parole officer or county judge or school principal, can require that every school report card be brought to him, can see about a part-time job for the boy. Thus many a lad with small opportunity might be won to Christ and the whole family turned toward Christ and the church.

Or a police officer may be mentioned in the newspapers as having performed some deed of bravery and integrity, or he may have been promoted for long and faithful service. How nice for him to receive a letter from the pastor, and perhaps a letter from some businessmen of the church on their own stationery, congratulating him, thanking God for honest and faithful officers of the law, reminding him that according to Romans 13, the officer of the law, the judge, and the ruler, are the ministers of God for good and that all good Christian people are grateful for his services. And if the man has been greeted kindly, and if he is not a regular attendant of some other church, perhaps he would be willing to be present in a Sunday morning or Sunday evening service at the church, and with a brief introduction by the pastor and greeted by an informal handshake by godly Christians! Now he has found friends who are for the work he is trying to do. He has an incentive to be a better man, and he would likely be open to a kindly invitation to the services and to a quiet and loving word about Jesus Christ, the Saviour whom he needs.

The newspaper reports a fire in a modest home. A poor family has nearly all their household goods destroyed. There are little children. Some kindly Christian women should call at once, and the family be provided with some temporary quarters. Someone buys clothes for the little ones. Someone else calls among the members and finds what furniture can be donated here and there from this home and that one for the family. And in many cases it will not be hard to get that family in Sunday school next Sunday if people love them enough and prove friendly enough. Oh, there are many, many people who can be reached for Christ if there is enough love and concern and attention.

After every funeral announced in the paper, all the immediate loved ones of the deceased who live locally might receive a warm letter of condolence by the pastor saying that he will pray God to comfort them, and they should remember how Christ loves them and is ever ready to comfort the brokenhearted and save all of those who will come to Him, and saying that if ever the pastor or church can be of help, will they call on him?

Every time a high school boy or girl wins a scholarship in college or young people win in a contest of the Future Farmers, or every time a woman's cooking or handiwork wins a prize at the county fair, it would be proper for Christian people representing Christ and the church to write a note of congratulation or to say it personally when that is convenient, and prove themselves friendly, and wherever there is an opportunity to say a word for Jesus Christ.

If Christians loved people enough, they would be glad when one is promoted. They would feel like praising those who do well. They would sincerely from the heart wish to comfort those who are bereaved. Oh, everybody is the business of pastor and church, and we should seek some contact with every heart in the community.

That person who has had an accident and is in the hospital may be an utter stranger. Whether that person be a Catholic or a Christian Scientist or an atheist, you may be sure that the bringing of some flowers or a book to read, with a handshake and offer to help and perhaps a prayer by the bedside, would be appreciated. There are few people who have lost loved ones who would not read gladly my little 64-page book with a lovely art cover, Bible Facts About Heaven. Someone gave a copy to Mrs. Henry Ford when her son, Edsel Ford, died. She wrote me in a black-bordered envelope a very gentle and sincere letter of thanks for the comfort and blessing it brought her in her bereavement.

Nearly every man in jail would be glad to read my booklet, "What Must I Do to Be Saved?" or a Christian magazine or other beautifully printed and attractive and readable Christian literature.

Usually, the friendship car or "Welcome Wagon" of the Chamber of Commerce will furnish a list of all the new people moving into the community, or the light company will give names and addresses of new people who have moved in. They are strangers. They do not yet have many friends. They would be glad for some kind person who wants them to come to church, and who wants to help the children get acquainted with others.

Not every advance will be received kindly. Not every witness will bear immediate fruit. Some seed will fall on stony ground and the birds of Satan will take some seed away. But some will fall on good ground. The church should set out to use every means available to meet and to love and to witness to every person in the community and beyond.

11. Our Churches' Sad Lack of Holy Spirit Power

In preceding chapters we have named some of the reasons why our churches win few souls or none. It is true that churches fail to win many souls because that is not the one program, the one all-consuming passion of the church. It is true that the failure of our preaching, of our music, our formal worship services, our lack of utilizing the Sunday school for soul winning, the lack of constant community-wide visitation program, are all part of the fruitlessness of our churches. But back of all these failures is the one basic and supreme failure: our churches do not have the fullness of power of New Testament churches. Most pastors and people are not filled with the Holy Spirit and so do not have miraculous, supernatural power upon their testimony.

I. Scriptural Motives, Orthodoxy and Methods All Fail Without God's Power

There are good churches, thousands of them in America, where the pastor believes the Bible and the people are generally converted, godly people, who want to see souls saved, and they even try to win souls but do not succeed because the pastor and the people are not filled with the Spirit.

D. L. Moody wisely said, "It is foolish to try to do the work of God without the power of God." The Apostle Paul said, "Our sufficiency is of God; Who also hath made us able ministers of the new testament; not of the letter, but of the spirit: for the letter killeth, but the spirit giveth life" (II Cor. 3:5, 6). Remember Paul speaks here, not of the ceremonial law, but of the "new testament." The Word of God Itself killeth unless It be in the power of the Spirit.

Thus there are churches and pastors who believe in the

inspiration of the Bible, the deity of Christ, His virgin birth, His bodily resurrection, His atonement on the cross, and even in His premillennial return, who go week in and week out, month after month, with never a soul saved! The letter even of orthodoxy is a deadening thing without the power of the Spirit of God. Orthodoxy set on fire by the Spirit of God can make a wonderful New Testament church, with multitudes saved. Orthodoxy without the power of God can make the church full of Pharisees, with few spiritual babies born or none. Dr. Bob Jones, Sr., well says, "It takes evangelistic unction to make orthodoxy function."

The Sunday school may have well-trained teachers. They may keep careful records, and that is essential. They may visit absentees, but unless the blessed Holy Spirit puts the compassion of Christ in the heart and moves with power on the teaching and on the witnessing and on the visitation by the teachers, it will be largely fruitless.

The musicians may sing the right songs, but unless they also fulfil, "Be filled with the Spirit; Speaking to yourselves in psalms and hymns and spiritual songs, singing and making melody in your heart to the Lord," as Ephesians 5:18, 19, commands us, there will be no saving power in the music either to convict or to decide the sinner for Christ.

There are churches and preachers who proudly announce that they are taking part in what they called "the charismatic revival," that is, influenced by Pentecostal people, they claim to seek the gifts of the Spirit. They talk in tongues. They have prayer for the sick. There are genuine gifts of the Spirit though we do not believe that usual "speaking in tongues" is what they had at Pentecost nor that it is a gift of the Spirit. We are not against a blessed moving of the Holy Spirit in giving gifts to God's people and manifesting Himself wonderfully in their lives. But to seek the gifts of the Spirit without being filled with the Holy Spirit for soul-winning power will still leave our churches barren and fruitless.

I am thinking now of an Episcopal church which I passed by regularly and the dance for young people on Friday night was followed by healing meetings on Sunday. But neither at the dance nor the healing meetings was an ingathering of lost souls.

Yesterday, a young Pentecostal ministerial student came to me with deep concern after I had preached on "The Power of Pentecost." He bought my book on The Power of Pentecost, and he said to me, "I am Pentecostal, but I think we Pentecostal people had better come back to keeping the cart behind the horse, and seek first of all soul-winning power."

I do not mean, then, that we should seek some climactic "experience" of joy for our own delight. I do not mean that we should now have a "second work of grace" or "entire sanctification," which would give us "perfect love," or eradicate the carnal nature. I am for holy living in the Bible sense, but our churches need something far more than this. We need the supernatural power of God in our witnessing.

I do not now mean that one should talk in tongues (foreign languages, which the word in such a connotation always means in the Bible). If there are none present who need the Gospel in a foreign language, then I see no sense in preaching to them in a foreign language. There was good reason to do so at Pentecost.

No, I mean what Jesus meant in Luke 24:46-49:

> "...Thus it is written, and thus it behoved Christ.to suffer, and to rise from the dead the third day: And that repentance and remission of sins should be preached in his name among all nations, beginning at Jerusalem. And ye are witnesses of these things. And, behold, I send the promise of my Father upon you: but tarry ye in the city of Jerusalem, until ye be endued with power from on high."

I mean that the churches and the preachers should claim

the promise of Jesus in Acts 1:8, "But ye shall receive power, after that the Holy Ghost is come upon you: and ye shall be witnesses unto me both in Jerusalem, and in all Judaea, and in Samaria, and unto the uttermost part of the earth."

II. Whole Church at Jerusalem Was "Filled With the Spirit"

It is true that God deals primarily with individuals. A person has to come personally to trust in Christ as Saviour, repenting of his sins and accepting the free gift of God. Prayer ought usually to be in secret, and so most of one's praying, I think, should be alone. Of course, we have cases of individuals who were personally filled with the Holy Spirit, one at a time.

So Jesus was filled with the Spirit in Luke 3:21, 22. So was John the Baptist in Luke 1:15, Elisabeth in Luke 1:41, Zacharias in Luke 1:67, Peter in Acts 4:8, Paul in Acts 9:17. But a church can be so united in a burden for souls and in pleading for God's power that the whole church group can be filled with the Holy Spirit.

So, it seems was the group that met in that Upper Room praying before Pentecost for the power of the Holy Spirit. Jesus had said to them, "But tarry ye in the city of Jerusalem, until ye be endued with power from on high" (Luke 24:49). And so we believe that the command to the little group that stayed together after the crucifixion was obeyed. In Acts 1:4, 5, we are told:

> "And, being assembled together with them, commanded them that they should not depart from Jerusalem, but wait for the promise of the Father, which, saith he, ye have heard of me. For John truly baptized with water; but ye shall be baptized with the Holy Ghost not many days hence."

And he continued in verse 8,

"But ye shall receive power, after that the Holy Ghost
is come upon you: and ye shall be witnesses unto me both
in Jerusalem, and in all Judaea, and in Samaria, and unto
the uttermost part of the earth."

And then in Acts 1:13, 14, the apostles are named and we
are told, "These all continued with one accord in prayer and
supplication, with the women, and Mary the mother of Jesus,
and with his brethren." There were other Christians in the
world, but this little congregation at least were of "one accord" in waiting for the power of God upon them to witness
and carry out the command of the Great Commission.

And in due time, "When the day of Pentecost was fully
come, they were all with one accord in one place" (Acts 2:1).
And there the little body, all of one mind and all praying together, "were all filled with the Holy Ghost" (vs. 4), we are
told.

I do not suppose that each one just happened to meet whatever requirements God made in waiting, and praying, but
the united prayers of the group had a power that individual
prayers alone did not have. And perhaps the lack of fervor
or faith on the part of one was made up by the fervor or
faith of another. I do not know. I just know that there, in a
great example which is portrayed for us of how the church
at Jerusalem started out to obey the Great Commission,
they with one accord waited and prayed and sought and found
a great enduement of power. And we read on to see that in
Acts 2:41, "Then they that gladly received his word were
baptized: and the same day there were added unto them
about three thousand souls." And then, "And the Lord added to the church daily such as should be saved" (Acts 2:47).
So the power of God upon them made them fruitful as a
whole congregation.

Individually, the power of God came upon Peter alone
when there was an occasion in Acts 4:8 when Peter addressed the rulers. But now there was a great threat to the

group. The apostles were commanded to preach no more in the name of Jesus, and they were straitly threatened, and went back "to their own company, and reported all that the chief priests and elders had said unto them" (Acts 4:23). And that group, again called "their own company" (so we suppose that it included in general the new converts as well as the original 120), "lifted up their voice to God with one accord" (vs. 24). They prayed, "Behold their threatenings: and grant unto thy servants, that with all boldness they may speak thy word, By stretching forth thine hand to heal; and that signs and wonders may be done by the name of thy holy child Jesus" (Acts 4:29, 30). And so again, the Holy Spirit came upon the whole group. "And when they had prayed, the place was shaken where they were assembled together; and they were all filled with the Holy Ghost, and they spake the word of God with boldness" (Acts 4:31).

It is important to notice that whatever happened essentially in Acts 2:4, happened again in Acts 4:31. In both verses are exactly the same nine words in our King James Version, "And they were all filled with the Holy Ghost." In one case, there was the sound of a cyclonic wind and visible "tongues like as of fire." In the other case, there was an earthquake and "the place was shaken"; but in both cases we read, "And they were all filled with the Holy Ghost." So again, and when there was need for power, the people prayed, and again the blessed Spirit of God came upon them.

I thank God that the blessed anointing and power of the Holy Spirit is renewable. If I need God's power to witness, I may have it. If I need God's power again to witness, I may have it. If God's local congregation can with one accord seek God in prayer and be all filled with the Holy Spirit, then the same congregation can again with one accord seek God in prayer and be filled with the Holy Spirit.

The church, then, had Spirit-filled preaching, Spirit-filled deacons, and Spirit-filled house-to-house witnessing.

III. Great Secret of Soul Winning Is Spirit-Filled Witnessing in Public and Private

The Bible takes particular pains to tell us that the Holy Spirit came on individuals at Pentecost. Peter reminded the people in his sermon there of the prophecy of Joel 2:28-32. In this New Testament age, called there "the last days," God had said, "I will pour out my Spirit upon all flesh: and your sons and your daughters shall prophesy, and your young men shall see visions, and your old men shall dream dreams: And on my servants and on my handmaidens I will pour out in those days of my Spirit; and they shall prophesy" (Acts 2:17, 18). So, on young and old, on men and women, on servants and handmaids, came the blessed power of the Holy Spirit, and the result was as foretold in the prophecy of Joel, "Whosoever shall call on the name of the Lord shall be delivered" (2:32).

Prophesying means witnessing in the power of the Holy Spirit and the result is to be that people will be saved. So we learn that Peter and Paul preached in the power of the Spirit. When Paul and Barnabas were sent away on their missionary journey, first, a little group of Christians waited and fasted and prayed before sending Paul and Barnabas away as the Holy Ghost had said for them to do. "So they, being sent forth by the Holy Ghost, departed unto Selucia" (Acts 13:4). And we are not surprised that at Paphos, on the Island of Cyprus, Paul would win the deputy Sergius Paulus and answer Elymas the sorcerer. We read, "Then Saul, (who also is called Paul,) filled with the Holy Ghost, set his eyes on him, And said..." (Acts 13:9, 10).

Then when Paul and Barnabas came to Iconium they "so spake, that a great multitude both of the Jews and also of the Greeks believed" (Acts 14:1). That means surely that they had upon them the miracle-working power of the Holy Spirit and spoke in His power.

So it had been with the preaching deacon, Stephen, full of the Holy Ghost. "And Stephen, full of faith and power, did great wonders and miracles among the people" (Acts 6:8). And then, facing martyrdom, with "the face of an angel" (vs. 15), Stephen preached. And when the mob were "cut to the heart and they gnashed on him with their teeth" (Acts 7: 54), "He, being full of the Holy Ghost, looked up stedfastly into heaven, and saw the glory of God, and Jesus standing on the right hand of God, And said, Behold, I see the heavens opened, and the Son of man standing on the right hand of God" (Acts 7:55, 56). Oh, for more Spirit-filled deacons to witness for Jesus!

The command, "Be not drunk with wine, wherein is excess; but be filled with the Spirit" (Eph. 5:18), is surely for every Christian. It is a sin to get drunk. It must be, according to the same verse of Scripture, equally wicked not to be filled with the Spirit of God. Our churches are fruitless because our pastors and deacons and teachers and members, are not filled with the Holy Spirit for witnessing.

IV. Our Churches Need to Make Room for the Holy Spirit

If we are to have churches and people filled with the Holy Spirit, then there must be much preaching on soul winning and on the power which God has promised for soul winners. There has been great confusion among Christian people on this issue. Pentecostal people put emphasis on talking in tongues. Holiness people teach a second work of grace and sanctification, and call it the fullness of the Spirit. The Plymouth Brethren group bring the teaching of John Nelson Darby into the Bible institutes and have turned the Bible institutes away from the scriptural teaching of D. L. Moody, R. A. Torrey and great soul winners of the past. It has become popular to say that Pentecost cannot be repeated. It has become the customary thing to emphasize not the three thousand souls saved at Pentecost, not the connection which Jesus Himself made between the Great Commission and the enduement of power, but to speak of Pentecost as the birthday of the church and make it purely a dispensational matter, without any practical value to the Christian today! How sad!

And the preacher who preaches on the fullness of the Spirit risks being misunderstood, risks even more being called a fanatic. Well, if he would please God and have the New Testament ministry, he must still preach what the Bible preaches, and teach that the great equipment for soul winning is the power of the Holy Spirit.

Some people teach baptismal regeneration: is that a reason to quit preaching Bible baptism and quit baptizing converts? Some people teach that one can have the carnal nature eradicated and so teach what I think is an extreme and a perverted position on holiness. But should Christian people seek to be no longer holy, and should preachers not preach that the body of the Christian is the temple of the Holy Ghost and should be kept holy, acceptable to Him, with reasonable service? All kinds of fanaticism and false doctrine have been taught in connection with the truth about the premillennial coming of Christ. Should Christians therefore not preach and not look for the blessed second coming of Christ? Are we to throw away "the blessed hope" because some false teachers have perverted the doctrine? Not so!

Well, how much more must we be faithful to teach and to have the power of God and to preach that Christians may be filled with the Spirit for soul-winning power, even though some have misused the terminology of the Holy Spirit. So, preacher, you may need to explain what you mean by "filled with the Spirit," but you should still command that people be filled with the Spirit, as the Bible commands it.

Christians should be taught to wait on God for Holy Spirit power. There ought sometimes to be a half night of prayer, as I experienced a good number of times in the People's Church in Toronto, or a whole night of prayer as we experienced in three separate nights in a city-wide campaign in Buffalo, New York, in 1945. Sometimes there should be a day of fasting and prayer when people go aside and miss meals while they wait on God and seek to have their lives cleaned up and their faith renewed and to seek a breath of Heaven upon them, a literal coming of God's power upon them for soul-winning witnessing. The church should make room for the Holy Spirit.

That means that in the services there must be a certain freedom. Suppose we have a formal worship service and the schedule is already printed. Then, oh, teach everybody that the Holy Spirit Himself must be director of the service and that it can be adjusted to His leading and to His purpose. The preacher must sometimes be free to stop in the midst of his sermon to give an invitation, if the Spirit of God tells him the time is now. Sometimes when the pleading invitation song pulls at the hearts of people and sinners are coming to Christ, the pastor must feel free to hold the crowd on beyond the noon hour and put soul winning before the bellies of carnal Christians who may be looking at their watches, anxious to get home to the big Sunday dinner. And in the music there must be room for the singer who may be unlettered but sings with lilt and joy and blessing, instead perhaps of the cultured professional with a worldly heart.

When God seems to be moving for revival, nothing must stand in the way. No choir picnic, no young people's social must draw the hearts and interest away from the soul-winning services. If the right kind of preparation and advertising and singing must cost money, then the money belongs to God and it must be spent to please Him as the Holy Spirit leads. Oh, the Holy Spirit must be the boss, and must have His way, if He is to have His power manifested in our churches.

Strange things may happen in the church where people are filled with the Spirit. Sometimes there will be amazing answers to prayer, unreasonable they will seem. God will stop the rain suddenly that the service may proceed. Or bring rain in a time of drought. Or a sick person will be given faith to trust the Lord and be wonderfully healed. Or

God may strike down some arrogant rebel who hinders revival and soul winning. Oh, I beg you, make room in your church for the work of the Holy Spirit, plead with Him to take over and let us make sure we make room for Him to work.

If the Holy Spirit has freedom, we are going to find poor people coming to the services, illiterate and sometimes trashy people, dirty people, transients. Take care that you let the Holy Spirit have His way. Let the church lose its much-vaunted prestige as a church of the cultured and the rich and become a great common people's church, where the Spirit of God moves freely and where in every service it is expected that people will claim Christ as Saviour and where between services the people witness in every house and home for Jesus.

There will be criticism. Strangely enough, there is little criticism of the cold, formal church with its funeral-like atmosphere, its cultured choir, its scholarly preacher, its sermonette and its abandonment of the prayer meeting and the Sunday night service. But let the fire of God come, then there will be criticism.

We should remember that the dear Lord Jesus went for many, many years to the synagogue in Nazareth with never a critical word. He was a model young man. He was called on to read the Scriptures in public, "as his custom was" because he was the best scholar and the best reader. But one day He appeared among them filled with the Holy Spirit and quoted Isaiah 61:1 and said, "This day is this scripture fulfilled in your ears." They wondered at the gracious words that proceeded from His mouth, but their anger arose and they set out that day to kill Him and rushed Him out to a hill and would have cast Him down that Hill of Precipitation to kill Him if they could! Oh, there will be criticism, perhaps persecution and misunderstanding, if the preacher and the people are filled with the Spirit and if He manifests Himself in the services. But if you are going to bear fruit in winning multitudes, the Holy Spirit must have His way.

I do not mean the disorder in the services, "For God is not the author of confusion" (I Cor. 14:33). I do not mean careless preparation of the sermons. The very best that every man has is none too good for the service of God. I do not mean that we should not try to have beautiful music and that we ought not to try to be reasonable and sensible as a part of godliness, but, oh, there must be a freedom for the Holy Spirit to have His way if our churches, our people and preachers are to be filled with the Spirit and win multitudes.

The Ruin of a Christian

REPROVES ... REBUKES ... EXHORTS

Tremendously popular book, by Evangelist John R. Rice, D.D., Litt.D.; 28,000 copies printed. These sermons are selected from ten years of writing. They have been preached all over America, reviving Christians and leading to consecration and soul winning. God has breathed on these messages. You need this book to warm your heart and perhaps to convict you of sin and transform your life into what God wants you to be.

CHAPTER TITLES

1. The Ruin of a Christian.
2. Lukewarmness — The Sin That Makes God Vomit.
3. God's Slaughter Crew.
4. The Curse of Hidden Sins.
5. The Sin of Lying.
6. "Break Up Your Fallow Ground, and Sow Not Among Thorns."
7. The Seven-Fold Sin of Those Who Do Not Win Souls.
8. "Speak Not Evil One of Another, Brethren."
9. Judge Not!
10. "Be Ye Not Unequally Yoked Together With Unbelievers."
11. Washing Dirty Feet.
12. A New Start.

Distinguished Comments—

CHRISTIAN HERALD —"*Here is evangelistic preaching with all the fine passion, humor and drama of Dwight Moody.*"

DR. HYMAN J. APPELMAN—"*Every chapter is eminently worthwhile . . . Without any reservation I recommend it unhesitatingly to everyone everywhere.*"

DR. JOE HENRY HANKINS, powerful Southern evangelist — "*The most powerful exposures of the most common and deadly sins among professing Christians everywhere today that I have read or heard.*"

DR. TORREY M. JOHNSON, long president Youth for Christ International—"*It will search, it will convict, it will challenge, it will heal, it will help bring revival.*"

DR. W. W. MELTON, past General Secretary Baptist General Convention of Texas —"*I do not know when I have read a book with more interest.*"

Sturdy cloth binding. Illustrated jacket. A good book buy.

253 pages ----------------------- **$2.50**

SWORD OF THE LORD PUBLISHERS

Box 1099   Murfreesboro, Tennessee

The Coming Kingdom of Christ

New revised edition of this famous classic on Bible prophecy.

by JOHN R. RICE, D.D., Litt.D.

An easy-to-understand, Scriptural, convincing, exhaustive study. Places prophecies in their proper perspective, shows that all the Scriptures of the Old and New Testaments fit into a simple, clear, understandable pattern of what God plans. No speculation, no guesswork or date setting, but the Scriptures explained.

With the Bible before him, the humblest, least scholarly Christian can see what God promises. The Scriptures are taken at face value, so that all who approach the study without bias can agree wholeheartedly with the principal doctrines Dr. Rice discusses. Will answer questions, comfort and bless, create a longing in your heart for the coming of the Saviour.

"Greatest Collation of Scripture on its theme since John Wilkinson issued 'Israel My Glory' over half a century ago"—Col. Rev. F. J. Miles

"Many books in these recent days have been written in defense of these truths, but we do not recall any that are more convincing" —Moody Monthly.

CHAPTER TITLES:

1. Blessings in the Study of Prophecy.
2. God's Covenant with Abraham: His Seed to Possess Canaan Forever.
3. Israel to Be Restored as a Nation.
4. When Will Israel Be Regathered and Converted? At Christ's Coming!
5. David's Kingdom Over Israel to Be Restored Forever.
6. Jesus to Be King of the Jews on David's Throne.
7. The Kingdom Postponed Until the King Returns.
8. The Kingdom of Christ on Earth Is Yet Future.
9. Eternal Promises to the City Jerusalem.
10. World-Wide Righteousness, Peace, and Prosperity Promised in Christ's Kingdom.
11. The Saved and Glorified to Reign with Christ on ⌐arth After His Coming.
12. Some Unsaved on Earth, in Natural Bodies During Millennium.
13. What Must Come Before the Kingdom—Looking for Jesus.
14. No Signs of Christ's Coming.
15. Get Ready for Christ's Coming.

Jacket drawn by famous artist especially for this book. Fifteen great chapters, 202 pages, beautiful cloth binding, --------------- **$2.50**

SWORD OF THE LORD PUBLISHERS

Box 1099   Murfreesboro, Tennessee

Do You Have the Power You Need?

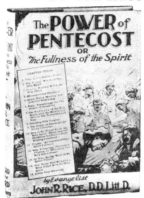

THE POWER OF PENTECOST

or

The Fullness of the Spirit

By JOHN R. RICE, D.D., Litt.D.

* * * The result of seventeen years of loving labor, by Dr. Rice, author of scores of helpful books and booklets. Here is the most important book on this subject to appear in 20 years.

The largest and most exhaustive study in print on soul-winning power. Full explanation of Pentecost: I Corinthians, chapter 14. Not the new teaching of the Darbyites and ultra-dispensationalists, but the old-time teaching of Moody, Torrey, Spurgeon, Finney.

A book of ripest scholarship, it avoids the pitfalls of false cults and extremists. No fanaticism. Solid Bible teaching, fervent, Spirit-filled application, quotations from famous Christians. Here you may actually learn what the fullness of the Spirit means, what it will do for you, how to have it.

441 pages, detailed indexing, beautifully bound. An important book for every soul winner and Christian worker. Price . . $3.50

Chapter Titles

1. The Lost Secret-Power
2. The Usual Work of the Holy Spirit
3. Jesus, Filled With the Holy Ghost
4. Misunderstood Pentecost
5. Spirit-Filled Means Empowered Witnessing
6. Bible Terminology for the Power of Pentecost
7. The Fullness of the Holy Spirit and the Ministry Gifts in Old Testament and New
8. Speaking with Tongues
9. The Power of Pentecost for Every Christian
10. How to Be Filled With the Holy Spirit
11. Prayer—A Condition of Holy Spirit Fullness
12. Why Prevailing, Persistent Praying Is Necessary for Holy Spirit Power
13. Do You Really Want to Be Spirit-Filled?
14. How Great Soul Winners Were Filled With the Holy Spirit
15. Claim Your Blessing

The Home: *Courtship, Marriage, and Children...*

During twenty-four years of pastoral, evangelistic and editorial work, Dr. Rice has been confronted with troubled folk of all ages, in private conversation, in letters by the thousand, and in forums, with questions on courtship and petting, child discipline, family altar, birth control, duties of husbands and wives, divorce, normal sex life in marriage and many other home problems. Thus he saw the need for a sane, biblical, understanding and practical book on the home and problems of married people. We believe he was eminently qualified to write it—by his experience, his deep and and burning devotion to the Lord, his undoubted Bible scholarship and his skillful writing.

An excellent wedding gift; every home should have a copy, every young person. Family record, marriage certificate. 22 long chapters, 381 pages in lovely cloth binding.

YOUR Choice! 3⁵⁰ a book

—America's Best-Seller on Prayer

200,000 Printed

The miracle-working God still answers prayers as He did in Bible times and for our fathers. Here one can learn how to pray in the will of God, grow in faith, really get things from God and live the joyful life of daily answered prayer. Commended by hundreds.

HYMAN J. APPELMAN says: "Last night I finished your marvelous book on Prayer. I say advisedly it is the very greatest thing of its kind I have ever read . . . Thank God for the Holy Spirit's using you to write every line of it."

Attractive paper jacket, beautifully cloth-bound, 328 large pages, 21 chapters.

SWORD OF THE LORD PUBLISHERS

Box 1099   **Murfreesboro, Tennessee**